Mirror Series A

漫譚中國

READ ABOUT CHINA

Pao-ch'en Lee

FAR EASTERN PUBLICATIONS
YALE UNIVERSITY
NEW HAVEN, CONNECTICUT

First Printing, 1953
by
Far Eastern Publications

Table of Contents

Introduction to First Edition v

Introduction to Second Edition viii

Lesson One: The History of China 1

Lesson Two: The Geography of China 7

Lesson Three: Chinese Inventions (1) 13

Lesson Four: Chinese Inventions (2) 18

Lesson Five: New Year Celebrations 23

Lesson Six: New Year Celebrations (continued) 29

Lesson Seven: Dragon-Boat and Mid-Autumn Festivals 35

Lesson Eight: Chinese Proverbs (1) 42

Lesson Nine: Chinese Proverbs (2) 48

Lesson Ten: How Chinese Are Named 54

Lesson Eleven: How Chinese Are Named (continued) 60

Lesson Twelve: The Family Concept 66

Lesson Thirteen: Religions in China (1) 72

Lesson Fourteen: Religions in China (2) 78

Lesson Fifteen: The Great Wall and the Grand Canal 85

Lesson Sixteen: What is Gwóyǔ (the Chinese National Language)? 92

Lesson Seventeen: The Four Tones of Gwóyǔ 99

Lesson Eighteen: The Chinese Written Language 106

Lesson Nineteen: Chinese Food 113

Lesson Twenty: Democracy and China 120

目　　次

第 一 課　中國的 Lìshř …………………………………… 一
第 二 課　中國的地 -lǐ …………………………………… 七
第 三 課　中國的發明（一） ………………………………… 一三
第 四 課　中國的發明（二） ………………………………… 一八
第 五 課　過年……………………………………………… 二三
第 六 課　接着過年………………………………………… 二九
第 七 課　五月-jyé 跟八月 -jyé ………………………… 三五
第 八 課　中國俗話（一） …………………………………… 四二
第 九 課　中國俗話（二） …………………………………… 四八
第 十 課　姓名問題………………………………………… 五四
第十一課　再談姓名問題…………………………………… 六十
第十二課　家-dzú 觀念……………………………………… 六六
第十三課　中國的宗教（一） ……………………………… 七二
第十四課　中國的宗教（二） ……………………………… 七八
第十五課　長城跟運河……………………………………… 八五
第十六課　甚麽是國語……………………………………… 九二
第十七課　國語四聲………………………………………… 九九
第十八課　中國文字………………………………………一〇六
第十九課　中國飯…………………………………………一一三
第二十課　民主 跟 中國……………………………………一二〇

INTRODUCTION TO THE FIRST EDITION

The English title of this book, READ ABOUT CHINA, is not an exact translation of the Chinese one, 漫談中國 (Màn Tán Jūnggwó) meaning "Chat About China". The justification for this difference is that while the writer was writing this book, he was really mentally chatting with his readers like friends over a cup of tea, free to talk about anything that interested them at the moment. Unfortunately, when this one-sided chat is published, it will become a book and the reader, who would not have had a chance to open his mouth during the chat anyway, will have to read about it.

This second-level text in Chinese characters is a continuation of the beginner's text, READ CHINESE, by Mr. Fang-yü Wang, and introduces another 300 characters to follow the 300 introduced in the first reader. The choice of these characters presented quite a problem. There have been a number of attempts to classify Chinese characters according to their usefulness. Some were based on extensive word counts, some highly subjective and some, merely composite lists based on previous check-lists. The choice of the 300 characters in this book is based first, on Dr. C. H. Fenn's first 1000 characters in his "Five Thousand Dictionary", Dr. Geoge A. Kennedy's composite list of 1020 Common Characters and the 1500 Common Characters newly announced by the Chinese Communist regime; and second, on the writer's own judgement. The question of the usefulness of characters is difficult to decide, because while characters like 鹽 (salt) or 糖 (sugar) are useful to housewives and probably should be included in the first 500 characters of their vocabulary, they are not quite as useful to those who want to read the Chinese newspaper as 發展 (develop) or 政府 (government). Moreover, most of the word counts were undertaken some years ago, so do not include some important ones in their first 1000 like 努 in 努力 (with all one's power) which has become widely used in recent years. This textbook is prepared for those preparing to read Chinese newspapers, magazines, etc. as soon as possible. With this goal in mind, the writer has chosen 300 characters according to their frequency in the above mentioned check-lists plus his own judgement, and they have been approved by the Editorial Committee of the Institute of Far Eastern Languages, Yale University.

Instead of the rebus method used in READ CHINESE, it is thought advisable to use Chinese characters all the way. The unrequired characters appearing in each lesson for the first time are explained in the Notes section of that lesson. Those repeated in later lessons are not explained again, nor are they given any cross reference. The student is asked to learn to count the number of strokes of the character in doubt (the first one in the case of a compound) and look it up in the index. Tackling these unrequired characters and looking them up may be time-consuming but not entirely time lost. In the writer's teaching experience, many a student has liked this method, for it helped him to learn the writing of Chinese characters more thoroughly and he has picked up new words for nothing, so to speak.

Fifteen required new characters are introduced in each of the twenty lessons. Useful compounds and phrases containing these new characters and those which they already know are listed and explained in the Vocabulary section of each lesson. Much effort has been spent to make the new characters appear at least once every third lesson, so that students will have a chance to refresh their memory from time to time. Since fifteen different topics have been discussed in this book, it has not been easy to do so. To remedy this, short sentences have been added at the end of each lesson except one, as supplementary reading material, utilizing those required characters which have not been repeated frequently enough in the main text. These sentences are in lighter vein and usually do not involve any unrequired characters. Although they do not necessarily dwell on the same topic as the lesson after which they appear, they do serve a specific purpose and should not be omitted in reading.

The writing of this book represents team-work. Without the aid, advice and encouragement of many persons, it would certainly never have been completed. Inadequate though his thanks may be, the writer would like to express his deep gratitude to a few of those who have helped: first, Professors Henry C. Fenn and George A. Kennedy who have offered invaluable advice in clarifying the Vocabulary and Notes; second, Dr. T'ien-yi Li and Mr. Fang-yü Wang who have carefully read and corrected the Chinese text; third, Mr. Fang-yü Wang who wrote Lesson Nineteen, Chinese Food, and the Chinese front cover; and finally, the writer's wife who not only wrote Lesson Fifteen, The Great Wall and the Grand Canal, and prepared the index, but also untiringly copied out all the Chinese characters in this book.

Pao-ch'en Lee

New Haven, Conn.

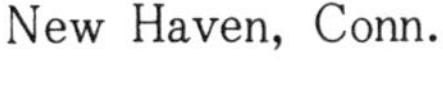

INTRODUCTION TO THE SECOND EDITION

After this book had been used at the U. S. Army Language School, Presidio of Monterey, California, for one year, it became apparent to the writer that it was a little more advanced both in style and content than it was intended. In order to bridge the gap between this book and READ CHINESE, to which the former is a sequel in the Chinese Reader series, three important changes have been made in this second edition:

1. The rebus method used in READ CHINESE has been adopted in this book and all the unrequired characters appear in romanization form in the text. However, these unrequired characters are also written out in character form in the NOTES section of each lesson for students' reference only.

2. The combinations in the VOCABULARY & NOTES section of each lesson have been reduced in number so that only the essential and immediately useful ones are included.

3. The text has been somewhat modified to eliminate part of the unrequired characters and simplify the style as much as possible to avoid more involved sentences.

It is sincerely hoped that through these changes, the reader will find more satisfaction in reading about China.

Like what was done in the first edition, much effort has been spent in controlling the frequency of appearances of the 300 characters introduced in this book. It has been possible to make each character appear at least once every third lesson, so that the reader will have a chance to refresh his memory of what has been learned from time to time. The 300 characters introduced in this book appear 2,826 times altogether. Their frequency of appearances is shown in the following table:

APPEARANCES	CHARACTERS	TOTAL APPEARANCES
Below 5 times	93 *	242
5 - 10 times	114	824
11 - 15 times	43	542
16 - 20 times	24	435
21 - 25 times	7	155
26 - 30 times	8	227
31 - 35 times	7	227
36 - 40 times	2	75
Over 40 times	2	99
TOTAL	300	2,826

*72 of these 93 characters (over 77%) are introduced in the last six lessons. Naturally, they do not have as many chances to reappear as the others introduced in earlier lessons.

Mr. Fred Wang, writer of READ CHINESE, did an admirable job in paralleling the vocabulary in his book with that of the last 12 lessons in SPEAK CHINESE, by Mr. M. Gardner Tewksbury. Unfortunately, the writer found it infeasible to do likewise with Mr. Wang's CHINESE DIALOGUES, a sequel to SPEAK CHINESE. The reason is that while the central theme in CHINESE DIALOGUES is: "Mr. Smith goes to Shanghai", the writer in this book talks about the various aspects of Chinese culture, which requires a different, though not necessarily a totally different, set of vocabulary. However, this book does have some relationship with CHINESE DIALOGUES, i.e., the vocabulary and sentence patterns already introduced in SPEAK CHINESE and CHINESE DIALOGUES are considered as having been learned and are not reintroduced any more in this book. Based on the practice that students learn two lessons a week, the following schedule has been observed in deciding what constitutes a new word or a new sentence pattern in this book:

SPOKEN CHANNEL		READING CHANNEL	
Textbook	Lessons	Textbook	Lessons
Speak Chinese	13, 14	Read Chinese	1, 2
	15, 16		3, 4
	17, 18		5, 6
	19, 20		7, 8
	21, 22		9, 10
	23, 24		11, 12
Chinese Dialogues	1, 2		13, 14
	3, 4		15, 16
	5, 6		17, 18
	7, 8		19, 20
	9, 10	Read About China	1, 2
	11, 12		3, 4
	13, 14		5, 6
	15, 16		7, 8
	17, 18		9, 10
	19, 20		11, 12
	21, 22		13, 14
	23, 24		15, 16
	— —		17, 18
	— —		19, 20

The writer is deeply grateful to Prof. Henry C. Fenn for his continued interest and encouragement; to Prof. Gerard P. Kok and Mr. Fred Wang for reading and correcting the text; to Dr. L. Carrington Goodrich for his suggestions to change some historical dates; to his former colleagues at the Yale Institute of Far Eastern Languages and his present ones at the U.S. Army Language School for their numerous suggestions.

Pao-Ch'en Lee

Carmel, California

漫 譚 中 國

第一課 中國的 Lìshř

中國是現在世界上一個最老的國家，已經有幾千年的 lìshř. 最早的 lìshř 因為沒寫下來，所以 lìshř-家說不是可 -kàu- 的 lìshř. 在 jìywán- 前差不多一千五百年的時候，中國就有了寫下來的 lìshř. 所以我們可以說中國可 -kàu- 的 lìshř 有三千五百年那麼長。

中國這幾千年有很多的 fā- 明。很多別的國家都有人到中國去學中國的文 -hwa. 從前中國人想中國是文 -hwà- 的中心，也是世界的中心，所以國家的名子叫中國。這一點兒也不奇怪。地中海叫地「中」海也是因爲從前西方人想地中海是世界中心的原故。

中國文 -hwà 是在中國北部黃河一帶生長起來的。後來 fājǎn-到中國的中部跟南部。

中國因爲有這麼多年的文 -hwà. 所以中國人從前多半總是喜歡舊的，不喜歡新的。舊的總是好，新的總是壞。連兩千五百年以前的 Kǔng-子都說，他只是 jyǎng 從前的學問，自己不 chwǎngdzàu 甚麼新的。

現在很多人－特別是 chīng- 年人－不這麼看了。他們覺得舊的裏頭有好有壞，新的裏頭也有好有壞。

中國在文 -hwa 方面是世界的國家裏一個老大哥；有很多可以給西方國家的東西。可是中國在別的方面也是一個小弟弟－特別是在 kē- 學方面－應當跟西方國家學。

（一）黃河的水特別極了，比甚麼河的水都黃。下一課再說是甚麼原故。

（二）中國西北部比海面高很多。

（三）洋火是從西洋來的，所以叫洋火。

（四）我們一共只有兩塊錢，只好別去了。

（五）我等了半天，連一個人也沒來。不知道是甚麼原故。

（六）美國的東邊兒是大西洋，西邊兒是太平洋。

（七）他總是喜歡到上海去。

（八）我們天天上 -wǔ 八點鐘上課，下 -wǔ 四點鐘下課。

（九）原來（本來）他常喝酒。現在不常喝了。

Vocabulary

No.	Character	Compound	Class	Meaning / Examples
1.	課 kè		M/N:	(for lessons)/school work
		上課	VO:	go to a class
		下課	VO:	class dismissed
				一. 今天我們念第十六課。
				二. 我們得去上課，五十分鐘以後就下課。
2.	世 shr̀		BF:	world; [generation; an age]*
3.	界 jyè		BF:	boundary
		世界	N:	the world
4.	海 hǎi		N:	sea
		地中海	PW:	the Mediterranean Sea
		上海	PW:	Shanghai
5.	原 ywán		BF:	origin; reason
		原來	MA:	originally (interchangeable with 本來)
				一. 原來他想到城裏去買東西，現在不去了。
6.	故 gù		BF:	reason; old
		原故	N:	reason
		故事	N:	story
7.	部 bù		M:	part, section
				一. 中國東部的人比西部的人多。
8.	黄 hwáng		SV:	be yellow (in color)
		黄河	PW:	the Yellow River
				一. 黄河的水很黄。
9.	總 dzǔng		A:	always (interchangeable with 老, and like 老, a 是 may be added: 總是)
				一. 他總(是) 說太忙，沒工夫。

* Square brackets are used for any meaning that is not pertinent to the immediate situation.

10. 連 lyán		CV:	even including, even
			一. 我連一塊錢也沒有。
11. 只 jř		A:	just, only (a 是 may sometimes be added: 只是)
	只好	A:	the best thing is to...
			一. 我不買這本書，我只是看看.
			二. 他還沒來,我只好一個人先吃飯了。
12. 特 tè		BF:	special(ly)
	特別	SV/A:	be special/specially
			一. 這個酒很特別，我特別喜歡喝。
13. 面 myàn		BF:	side; surface (interchangeable with 頭 in 前頭,後頭,上頭,下頭,裏頭 and 外頭)
	方面	N:	phase, aspect, side
	海面	N:	sea-level; surface of the sea
			一. 法國方面希望中國幫忙。
			二. 這個房子上面是白的,下面是黑的。
14. 洋 yáng		N/BF:	ocean/foreign
	大西洋	PW:	the Atlantic Ocean
	太平洋	PW:	the Pacific Ocean
	洋火	N:	matches
	西洋	PW:	the West
15. 共 gùng		BF:	altogether; to share
	一共	MA:	altogether, in all

Notes

1. 國家 N: country, nation
2. lìshř (歷史)* N: history

   lìshř-家 N: historian (家 is a suffix indicating a specialist in his field, equivalent to the English -ist, -ian, etc.)
3. 可-kǎu (靠) SV: be reliable
4. jìywán-前 (紀元-) TW: jìywán means the beginning of a reign or of an era—jìywán-前 is now understood as B. C.

   jìywán-後 TW: now understood as A. D.
5. fā-明 (發-) V/N: invent/invention
6. 文-hwà (-化) N: culture, civilization
7. 中心 N: center—from 中 (central) and 心 (heart)
8. 名子 N: name—from 名 (name) and 子 (an enclitic, a noun-suffix)
9. 西方 PW: the West—from 西 (west) and 方 (side), often interchangeable with 西洋
10. 帶 M: district, region, area

    在……一帶 Ph: in the region of...
11. 生 長 shēngjǎng V: grow, develop—from 生 (be born) and 長 (grow up)—note the character 長 reads jǎng here and not cháng
12. fājǎn (發展) V/N: develop/development
13. Kǔng-子 (孔-) N: Confucius—from 孔 (surname) and 子 (complimentary designation of men; a philosopher). When 子 is used for

*Chinese characters in parentheses are for reference only and not required for recognition.

this purpose, it is always given its full low-tone value and not like the 子 in 棹子, 兒子, etc.

14. jyǎng (講) V: explain, talk

15. 學問 N: learning – from 學 (learn) and 問 (to inquire)

16 chwǎngdzàu (創造) V: create

17. chīng-年人 (青-) N: young people

18. 有好有壞 IE: (It) has (its) good and bad (points)

19. 老大哥 IE: a senior brother (a courteous title to older people of the same generation)

20. kē-學 (科-) N: science

Gate of Heavenly Peace
Tyān Ān Mén, Běijīng

第二課　中國的地-lǐ

世界七大-jou 裏最大的jōu是Yǎjou. Yǎjou最大的國是中國。中國有差不多三百八十多萬方yīnglǐ,比Yǎjou-的四分-jr̄-一還大。中國人口一共有八萬萬人，差不多是世界人口的四分-jr̄-一。

中國除了兩個大平原以外,差不多都是山地。高山都在西部。兩個大平原，一個在北部，一個在中部。北部的平原在黃河一帶，中部的平原在長江一帶。

長江跟黃河是中國兩條最大的河。長江長三千一百yīnglǐ. 因爲是中國最長的河，所以叫長江。長江在全世界是第三條最長的河。黃河的水不乾淨。水裏有很多黃-ní, yánsher 總是黃的，所以叫黃河。黃河長兩千七百yīnglǐ, 比長江短四百yīnglǐ. 中國南部只有一條大河。跟長江黃河比起來短得多了。才有一千二百多yīnglǐ。

中國的幾個大湖都在長江一帶。因爲河裏的ní都lyóu-到這些湖裏去，所以湖水不很shēn, 只能走小船。

中國最大的城是上海；有四百九十多萬人；是世界第四個大城。上海是中國最大的海口；是中國的商業中心。第二個大城是天-jing;是中國北部的商業中心；有四百七十多萬人。北-jīng是第三個大城；有四百六十多萬人。因爲很多有名的大學都在北-jīng,所以北-jīng是中國教-yù-的中心。北-jīng是中國這六七百年的國-dū. 國民黨在一九二八年把國-dū bān-到南-jīng去以後，把北-jīng的名子gǎichéng北平。一九四九年共產黨把國-dū bān-回北平去的時候，又把名子gǎichéng北-jīng.

中國的地方這麽大，人這麽多，又有這麽多年的lìshř,真是世界上一個大國。現在雖然暫時不tǔng-一,可是我們準知道不久就要再byànchéng一個tǔng一的大國。

（一）我們很久沒見了。明天我準去看你。

（二）除了這個還不大乾淨以外，別的全都洗乾淨了。

（三）他總是喜歡聽故事，特別是可怕的故事。

（四）我暫時不打算作甚麽，連學校也不打算去了。

（五）他連太平洋在甚麽地方都不知道。

（六）上海是中國一個大海口，人口很多。

（七）請進來，別站在門口兒。

（八）請問這個地方都出產甚麽。

Vocabulary

1. 口 kǒu BF: mouth; an opening
   - 人口 N: population
   - 海口 N: seaport
   - 門口兒 PW: entrance, a doorway
2. 除 chú BF: besides, except
   - 除了… Ph: excepting ,not counting
   - …以外 一. 除了上海以外，別的地方我都沒去過。
3. 江 jyāng N: river (generally refers to a large one)
   - 長江 PW: the Yangtze River
4. 全 chywán A/SV: all, entirely/be complete, whole
   - 全都 A: entirely, completely, every one (more forceful than 都 alone)
     - 一. 這一課書我全懂了。
     - 二. 這個報不全，還有一張找不着了。
     - 三. 全世界的人差不多一半是男人，一半是女人。
     - 四. 這個屋子裏的人全都是我好朋友。
5. 乾 gān BF/[SV]: clean/[be dry]
6. 淨 jìng BF: clean
   - 乾淨 SV: be clean
7. 湖 hú N: lake
8. 商 shāng BF: trade, commerce
   - 商人 N: a merchant
9. 業 yè BF: business
   - 商業 N: business, commerce
10. 民 mín BF: people

人民 N: the people

一. 一個國家要是沒有人民，就不是一個國家了。

11. 黨 dǎng N: party (political)

國民黨 N: the Chinese Nationalist Party

12. 產 chǎn BF: product ; property

共產黨 N: the Communist Party

出產 V/N: produce

一. 去年美國出產的車比從前多。

二. 茶是中國的出產。

13. 暫 jàn BF: briefly, temporarily

暫時 MA: temporarily

一. 他們兩個人暫時在我家住。

14. 準 jwǔn A/SV: certainly/be accurate

一. 你請我喝酒，我準來。

二. 我的表不準。

15. 久 jyǒu BF: be long in time

不久 MA: before long

很久 SV: be a long time

很久沒見 IE: "Long time no see."

一. 我住了不久就走了。

二. 他在學校等了很久。

三. 王先生，很久沒見。

Notes

1.	地 -lǐ (-理)	N:	geography
2.	jōu (洲)	N:	continent
	七大 -jōu	Ph:	the continents of the world are usually referred to in this literary style without 個 after 七 as in the spoken style
3.	Yǎjōu (亞洲)	PW:	Asia—from 亞 (abbreviation of Yǎsyìyǎ which is the transliteration of Asia) and 洲 (continent)
4.	方 -lǐ (-哩)	M:	square mile—from 方 (square) and 哩 (mile). 哩 is a comparatively recently coined character, differentiating the English mile from the Chinese lǐ (里) which is about one-third of a mile.
5.	四分 -jr̄ 一 (-之-)	Nu:	one fourth—the fraction $\frac{x}{y}$ is expressed in Chinese as y-fēnjr̄-x, from 四 (four) 分 (part) 之 (of—the literary equivalent of 的) and 一 (one), meaning: of four parts, one.
6.	平原	N:	plain (geographical)—from 平 (level) and 原 (plateau)
7.	山地	N:	hilly country
8.	ní (泥)	N:	mud
9.	lyóu (流)	VV:	flow
10.	天 -jing (-津)	PW:	Tientsin—津 alone is pronounced jīn

11.	北平	PW:	Peiping—from 北 (northern) and 平 (peace)
12.	教-yù (-育)	N:	education— 教 is pronounced <u>jyàu</u> here
13.	國-dū (-都)	N:	capital of a country—note 都 is pronounced <u>dū</u> here
14.	北-jīng (-京)	PW:	Peking—from 北 (northern) and 京 (capital)
15.	南-jīng (-京)	PW:	Nanking—from 南 (southern) and 京 (capital)
16.	gǎichéng (改成)	RV:	change into
17.	統 tǔng	BF:	control
	統一	V/N:	unify/unity 一. 統一中國不是一件容易事。
18.	swéi-然 (雖-)	MA:	although
19.	byànchéng (變成)	RV:	become, change into—sometimes interchangeable with gǎichéng
20.	可怕	SV:	be productive of fear; be feared

The Li River, Gwèilín

第三課　中國的發明（一）

我們在第一課裏說過中國這幾千年有很多的發明。在這一課我們先講兩種很早的發明，就是dzàu sž 跟tsźchi.

Dzàu sž 的發明很早。Jyù-說是四千五百年以前發明的。到了兩千多年以前，中國的sž 才傳到外國去。最先是傳到Lwómǎ; 後來又從Lwómǎ 傳到別的國裏去。又過了一千多年，外國人才會dzàu sž. 現在除了中國以外，dzàu sž 最多的國家是意大-lì, 法國跟日本。意大-lì 就是從前的Lwómǎ.

sž很亮，很好看，可是很貴。現在雖然有了便-yi一點兒的人-dzàusž, 可是不像天然-sž 那麽好。所以女人還是喜歡買天然-sž 作衣-shang. 從前中國出口的東西裏，sž佔第一位。每年出的sž 大部分都運到外國去。

中國第二種很早的發明是tsźchi, 也有很久的lìshř 了。中國在Hàn Cháu 的時候就有了tsźchi. 後來作tsźchi 的法子越來越進-bù. 到了Chīng Cháu 的時候，已經發-jǎn-到最高的chéngdu, 没法子再進-bù 了。中國作tsźchi 最有名的地方是江西的Jǐngdéjèn. 那兒的tsźchi 作的非常好。常有時候要經過七十多人的手才能把一件tsźchi作好。所以中國的好tsźchi非常貴。

爲甚麽中國tsźchi這麽好呢？一個原故是因爲中國人特別喜歡喝茶，喝酒，並且非常講-jyou吃飯。講-jyou吃喝的人一定也講-jyou吃喝用的茶-bēi，酒-bēi跟飯-wǎn.

在一千年以前就有商人把中國tsźchi運到Ōujou去了。因爲很不容易運，所以非常貴。Ōujou最有錢的人才能買幾件tsźchi. 從前Ōujou不會作tsźchi. 所有的tsźchi都是從中國運去的。Tsźchi的Yīng-文名子是chinaware就是因為這個原故。現在世界各國都會作tsźchi了，可是我敢說還是中國tsźchi最好。

（一）這個地方前面是海，後面是山，並且很乾淨，真是一個好地方。

（二）我越來越不敢喝茶——特別是晚上——一喝茶就睡不着覺。

（三）他的運氣真好！走了半天還沒有人佔他的地方。

（四）那個鋪子各樣兒東西都很全，都是從西洋運來的。

Vocabulary

1. 發 fā BF: put forth, develop
   發明 V/N: invent/invention (lit. develop and bring to light)
   一. 火車是誰發明的?
   二. 這個是張先生的發明。
2. 講 jyǎng V: explain, talk
   一. 請你把他說的話講給我聽。
   二. 這位先生講書講的很好。
3. 種 jǔng M: kind, species
   一. 我不喜歡看這種書。
4. 傳 chwán V: transmit
   一. 這些話是誰傳給你的?
5. 雖 swéi BF: although
   雖然 MA: although
   一. 雖然你不喜歡我，我還是喜歡你。
6. 像 syàng V/SV: resemble, look like/be similar
   好像 A: a good deal like, it seems that
   一. 你看這孩子像誰?
   二. 他們兩個人很像。
   三. 他好像要睡覺。
7. 亮 lyàng SV: be bright, glossy, lustrous
   一. 屋子裏頭比屋子外頭亮。
8. 佔 jàn V: occupy
   一. 他佔了我的地方了。
9. 運 yùn V/BF: transport/luck
   運氣 N: luck, fortune
   有運氣 SV: be lucky, fortunate
   一. 我們走以前，得把東西先運走。

二. 王太太很有運氣；我的運氣壞極了。

10. 越 ywè A: still more

越來越…Ph: more and more……

越…越…Ph: the more……the more……

一. 那個飯舘兒的買賣越來越好。

二. 房子越大越好；錢越多越好。

11. 敢 gǎn AV: dare

不敢當 IE: You flatter me!, I do not deserve

一. 誰敢去？

二. 不敢當，我的中國話說的不好。

12. 並 bìng BF/P: and, also/(an intensive particle before a negative)

一. 他說他去，可是他並沒去。

13. 且 chyě BF: moreover; for the time being

並且 MA: moreover

暫且 MA: temporarily

一. 我們不但白天上課，並且晚上還要念書。

二. 我母親暫且跟我們一塊兒住。

14. 非 fēi BF: be not

非常 A: unusually

非…不可 Ph: insist on……, must (be)……

一. 他走得非常快。

二. 這件事非你辦不可。

15. 各 gè Sp: each, every

一. 城裏頭那個鋪子賣各種畫兒。

Notes

1.	dzàusz̄ (造絲)	VO:	the manufacturing of silk
2.	tsźchi (瓷器)	N:	chinaware
3.	jyù-說 (據-)	IE:	it is said (according to what is said)
4.	最先	MA:	at the very first
5.	Lwómǎ (羅馬)	PW:	Rome
6.	意大-lì (-利)	PW:	Italy
7.	人-dzàusz̄ (-造絲)	N:	artificial silk (lit. man-made silk)
8.	天然-sz̄ (-絲)	N:	natural silk—from 天然 (natural) and 絲 (silk)
9.	出口	V/N:	export/exportation—from 出 (go out) and 口 (port) 一. 中國出口的茶有很多運到美國來。
10.	位	M:	(for position)
11.	大部分	N:	the greater part
12.	Hàn Cháu (漢朝)	N:	the Han Dynasty (206 B.C.—220 A.D.)
13.	進-bù (-步)	SV:	be progressive
14.	Chīng Cháu (清朝)	N:	the Ching Dynasty (1644 A.D.—1911 A.D.)
15.	chéngdu (程度)	N:	degree, grade
16.	江西	PW:	Kiangsi province
17.	Jǐngdéjèn (景德鎮)	PW:	Ching-te-chen (a town in Kiangsi)
18.	講-jyou (-究)	V:	care a great deal about
19.	吃喝	N:	feasting
20.	bēi (杯)	N:	cup
21.	飯-wǎn (-碗)	N:	rice bowl
22.	Ōujou (歐洲)	PW:	Europe—from 歐 (abbreviation of Ōulwóbā which is the transliteration of Europe) and 洲 (continent)

第四課　中國的發明（二）

中國除了前一課講的造sz̄跟tsźchi這兩種發明以外，還有兩種在文-hwà-上非常重要的發明，就是造紙跟yìnshwā.這兩種發明對於整個世界的文-hwa都有很大的gùngsyàn.

在紙沒有發明以前，寫字的法子很多，可是都非常不方便。到了紀-ywán-後第一世紀Hàn Cháu的時候，中國有一個人發明了造紙的法子，能用樹皮造出紙來。到了第十二世紀的時候，中國造紙的法子才傳到Ōujou去。現在不但寫信畫畫兒跟yìn-書都一定要用紙，並且連在天天的生活裏也離不開紙。

Yìnshwā-的發明也有一千多年的lìshř了。最先作書都是用手寫，不能yìnshwā.後來在Hàn Cháu的時候，有了把字刻在石頭上的法子。刻好了以後，把紙放在石頭上，用mwò在紙上tù.沒字的地方就都變成黑yánsher；有字的地方還是白的。這可以說是yìnshwā-的第一步。到了第八世紀的時候，才把字刻在木頭上。每一-yè要刻一張木-bǎn.要是一本書有一百-yè，就要刻一百張木-bǎn.這種法子現在聽着雖然很bèn，可是這是中國 yìnshwā-上的一個大進步。

到了第十一世紀Sùng Cháu的時候，進了一步，發明了活字yìnshwā. 一個一個的字分開刻。yìn-的時候放在一塊兒。這跟現在的yìnshwā差不多了。

Yìnshwā傳到Ōujou是在第十五世紀明Cháu的時候。據說，Ōujou第一個用活字yìnshwā的是一個Dé-國人。在紀-ywán-後一四五-líng-年才用活字yìn書。這麽說起來，中國的活字yìnshwā比Ōujou的早了四個世紀呢。

我們在這一課跟上一課裏一共講了中國四種發明。中國還有很多別的發明，對於全世界的gùngsyàn也都很大。因爲我們還要談中國別的方面的事情，所以就不再談中國的發明了。

（一）自從Sùng Cháu以後，長江一帶的商業越來越進步。

（二）我準知道這只是暫時的，不會很久的。

（三）他總是說住在海邊兒上沒有住在湖邊兒上那麽好。湖邊兒上樹又多，水又乾淨。

Vocabulary

1. 造 dzàu　　V: manufacture, build
   一. 他在上海造了一個大房子。
   二. 中國很久以前就會造紙。
2. 重 jùng　　SV: be heavy; important
   重要　SV: be important
   一. 那個大鐘很重。
   二. 這本書很重要,我們都應當買一本。
3. 於 yú　　L: in, on, at, with reference to
   關於　CV: concerning, in respect to…
   對於　CV: as to…, in relation to…, (attitude) towards
   一. 我不願意知道關於他們兩個人的事情。
   二. 我對於唱歌兒一點兒都不懂。
4. 整 jěng　　BF: the whole
   整個　N: whole
   一. 這個東西我整個不喜歡。
5. 紀 jì　　BF: record, annals
   世紀　N: century
6. 樹 shù　　N: tree
7. 皮 pí　　N: bark, skin, leather, fur
   樹皮　N: bark
   一. 那件皮大衣是王先生給他買的。
   二. 用樹皮造紙是中國人發明的。
8. 活 hwó　　V/SV: live/be alive; moveable
   生活　V/N: live/life (in the sense of the condition of life), livelihood
   活字　N: moveable type

一. 他生氣的時候常說:「活着沒意思」。

二. 活字 yìnshwā 他是中國發明的。

9. 石 shŕ BF: stone

石頭 N: stone

10. 變 byàn V: become, change

一. 張先生說:「現在中國甚麽都變了」。

11. 成 chéng RVE/SV: complete/be O.K., satisfactory

變成 RV: change into, become

成不成? Ph: will it do or not?, O.K.?

一. 有一個男人現在已經變成女人了。

二. 只有錢不成, 還要有學問。

三. 我想用你的 chì-車, 成不成?

12. 步 bù M: step, pace

進步 V/N: progress

一. 先生們覺得我們進步得很快。

13. 木 mù BF: wood

木頭 N: wood

14. 據 jyù CV: according to

據說 IE: it is said

據他說 Ph: according to what he says

一. 據說他太太唱歌兒唱得很好。

二. 據他說中文很容易學。

15. 談 tán V: chat; talk about

談話 VO: carry on conversation

一. 請你到我家來談談好嗎?

二. 對不起, 我現在沒工夫談話。

Notes

1. yìnshwā (印刷) V/N: print/printing—from 印 (print) and 刷 (to brush, which was one of the procedures in block printing)
2. gùngsyàn (貢獻) V/N: contribute/contribution—a synonym compound, meaning to offer up to a superior
3. yìn-書 (印-) VO: the printing of books
4. kē (刻) V: engrave (same character as the 刻 in 一刻鐘)
   一. 在石頭上刻字很不容易。
5. mwò (墨) N: ink; ink-stick
6. tú (塗) V: smear
7. yè (頁) M: (for leaf and page of a book)
8. 木-bǎn (-板) N: wooden board
9. Sùng Cháu (宋朝) N: the Sung Dynasty (960—1278 A.D.)
10. 分開 RV: separate
    一. 這兩件事你應當分開作。
11. 明 Cháu (朝) N: the Ming Dynasty (1368—1643 A.D.)
12. 自從…以後 Ph: ever since (from……and thereafter)
    一. 自從他走了以後,我就沒再看見他。

第五課　過年

中國最重要的jyé是新年，最熱鬧的jyé也是新年。恐怕比西方國家的Shèngdànjyé還熱鬧。中國的新年跟陽-lì的一月一號不是一個時候。陰-lì的正月chū-一總是在陽-lì的一月最後十幾天，hwò-是二月頭十幾天。中國人一進Là-月就預備過年。一直過到正月十八才算過完了年。所以可以說中國人過年差不多要過兩個月。

Là-月chū-八那天，家家都喝Là-八-jōu. Là-八-jōu是用各種mǐ跟一些別的東西作的。吃的時候放上táng，很好吃。Là-月二十三那天jì dzàu. 據說家裏的Dzàu-王在這一天要到天上去報告這家一年所作的事情。因爲這個原故，所以要jì Dzàu-王，希望他多說幾句好話。

到了新年前幾天就更忙了。不但要預備過年吃的菜，還要把所有的屋子都shōushr-乾淨。街上也更熱鬧了。各地方都是紅紅lyù-lyù，非常好看。街上的人多極了：買東西的買東西，看熱鬧的看熱鬧。並且人人都要在新年以前lǐfǎ.

新年在中國是家裏的人在一塊兒過的jyé. 一家人平常也許分在幾個地方作事。可是在新年以前都要回家，在一塊兒過年。到一年最後的一天，一切事情都預備好了的時候，就把家裏的大門關起來，用紅紙把門封上，不叫家裏的好運氣跑出去。用紅紙的原故是因爲紅 yánsher 代表好運氣。封了門以後，一家人就在一塊兒接 shén, jì dzǔ-先。這些事都完了以後，就給父母長-bèi 拜年。拜完了年以後，一家人就又吃又喝，又說又笑，一夜不睡覺。

(一) 據說人在没飯吃的時候，也可以吃樹皮。

(二) 他現在變成一個很壞的人。他要是總是這樣，恐怕就没有希望了。

(三) 站在門口兒的那個人，像不敢進來的樣子。

(四) 請你代表我到車站去接黃世民先生去罷。我今天特別忙。

(五) 美國的七月四號也像中國過年的時候那麽熱鬧嗎？大家也整夜不睡覺嗎？

(六) 請一切都放心。張先生走以後，我一定常來看你。

(七) 那塊大石頭亮得很，特別是有太陽的那部分。

Vocabulary

1. 熱 rè SV: be hot
   一. 今天熱極了。
2. 鬧 nàu V: make a disturbance
   熱鬧 SV/N: be bustling, lively/excitement
   一. 昨天城裏頭熱鬧極了。
   二. 別鬧了，應當念書了。
3. 恐 kǔng BF: be afraid
   恐怕 MA: probably, perhaps
   一. 現在已經很晚了，恐怕他不來了。
4. 陰 yīn SV/BF: be shady, dark, cloudy/female principle in nature (opposite of 陽)
   陰天 N/VO: cloudy day/weather becomes cloudy
   一. 今天是陰天。
   二. 已經陰了三天了。
5. 陽 yáng BF: male principle in nature (opposite of 陰)
   太陽 N: the sun
6. 號 hàu M: day (of month); number (of house, room, telephone, etc.)
   一. 今天是十月十號。
   二. 我住在二十三街三百八十號。
7. 預 yù BF: in advance, beforehand
8. 備 bèi BF: prepare
   預備 V: prepare
   一. 明天上課以前，要把第六課預備好。
9. 希 syī BF: hope
10. 望 wàng BF: hope; [look at]
    希望 V/N: hope

一. 我希望到法國去住一個月。

二. 這只是一個希望。

11. 紅 húng SV: be red

臉紅 Ph: blushing

一. 他的臉很紅，一定又喝酒了。

二. 他還沒說話就臉紅了。

12. 切 chyè BF: all, entirely

一切 N: the whole lot

一. 一切的事都是他一個人作的。

13. 封 fēng V/M: seal/(for letters)

封上 RV: seal up

信封兒 N: envelope

一. 母親寫了三封信要我回家。

二. 請你把信封兒封上。

14. 代 dài BF: take the place of

代表 V/N: represent/representative

一. 我不願意代表你去。

二. 他是美國的代表。

15. 接 jyē V: welcome; meet some one at the station or dock; receive; continue (reading, speaking, etc.)

一. 我現在去接王小姐。

二. 昨天我接到我女朋友一封信。

三. 請接着念。

Notes

1. 過年 VO: pass the new year
   一. 你們過年過得很熱鬧吧。
2. jyé (節) N: festival
3. Shèngdánjyé (聖誕節) N: generally refers to Christmas, the complete form of which is Yēsū (Jesus) Shèngdàn (Holy Birthday)
4. 陽-lì (-曆) N: the solar calendar—from 陽 (sun) and 曆 (calendar)
5. 陰-lì (-曆) N: the lunar calendar—from 陰 (moon, which is also known as 太陰, the Great Female) and 曆 (calendar)
6. 正月 chū-一 (初-) TW: Chinese New Year's Day—all lunar months are called by their respective numbers followed by 月 except the lst and 12th which are called jēngywè (正 月) and làywè (臘 月) respectively and are seldom referred to by their respective numbers. The first ten days of each lunar month are referred to by their respective numbers with an ordinalizing prefix chū-, thus: chūyī, chūèr, chūsān, etc. All the other days of each lunar month are referred to by their respective numbers only, thus: shŕyī, shŕèr, shŕsān, etc.
7. 算 (是) V: consider as
   一 你必得會寫這個字才算(是)你真認

識這個字。

8. là-八(兒)-jōu (臘) (粥) N: gruel eaten on the 8th day of the 12th lunar month

9. mǐ (米) N: hulled rice, grain, uncooked rice

10. jì dzàu (祭竈) VO: sacrifice to the Kitchen god on the 23rd of the 12th lunar month—from jì (sacrifice to) and dzàu (kitchen-stove)

Dzàu-王 (竈-) N: Kitchen god—from dzàu (kitchen-stove) and wáng (ruler, king)

11. 報告 V/N: report—a synonym compound

一. 這件事你應當報告給學校。

二. 這件事你應當給學校作一個報告。

12. 所 L: that which (the combination 所+V means "that which is V'd")

一. 你所說的話全都不對。

13. 紅紅-lyùlyù(-綠綠) N: a gay colored sight (lit. red and green)

14. lǐfǎ (理髮) VO: get a haircut

15. 接-shén (-神) VO: welcome the gods

16. jì dzǔ-先 (祭祖-) VO: sacrifice to the ancestors

17. 長-bèi (-輩) N: seniors, those of one or more generations above—from jǎng (senior) and bèi (generation)

18. 拜年 VO: pay one's respects at New Year

一. 他出去拜年去了，一會兒就回來。

19. 整夜 N: the whole night

20. 部分 N: part, section

第六課　接着過年

過年的時候，天天夜裏聽見放花-pàu-的聲音。本來因爲中國人信gwěi怕聲音，所以過年的時候放pàu，各樣的gwěi就不敢來了。當然小孩子們最喜歡放花放pàu.所以後來花-pàu就變成了過年所不可少的東西。有時候放一整夜的pàu，連覺也不能睡。你越想睡覺，外面放pàu-的聲音越大。没法子！要過年就不能睡覺。當然過年的時候不想睡覺的還是佔大多數。

新年第一天，第一件事就是把昨天封上的門開開，讓新年帶來的好運氣進來。開門出去一看，各家門上都tyē-着寫着字的紅紙。上頭寫的都是像「一rù新年fú在yǎn-前」這一類的話。這一天街上的鋪子都關門休息，不作買賣。一直到chū-六才開開一半門，非正式的作買賣。街上的人很少。看見的人多半是出去拜年的男人。女人在這一天不能出去，因爲要是出去，家裏的運氣就帶出去了。

新年以後還不算過完了年呢。因爲正月十五那天是有名的燈jyé。各鋪子都在新年那十幾天裏作各種花燈。多半都是用紙作的。樣子越特別越好。到了十三十四十五那三天，各鋪子都gwà-出來，看誰的最好看。最普通的一種燈叫走馬燈。點起來的時候，有紙作的馬跟一些別的dùngwu在燈裏jwàn-來jwàn去。燈-jyé的時候，街上的燈雖然没有電燈那麼亮，可是因爲多，所以還是很亮。看燈的人真是人山人海，熱鬧極了。

到了正月十八那天，各鋪子就都把燈收起來，正式的又開門作買賣。吃喝玩兒lè休息了這麼多天。大家又都回到平常的工作。有的人已經希望很快的再到過年的時候。也許有人覺得真是謝天謝地！新年過了，又可以gwēigweijyujyū-的作事了。

我們在這兩課裏所講的都是一些過年最普通的事。中國地方這麼大，人這麼多，各地方過年一定不大一樣。不一樣的地方，我們就不在這裏談了。

（一）這種紅花恐怕很貴。你還是買那種黃的罷。

（二）據他說，美國人很普通的事情也打電報。

（三）馬先生收到朋友給他的一封信，說馬太太預備明年春天回國。

（四）别叫小孩子玩兒洋火。

Vocabulary

1. 花 hwā N: fireworks ; flower
   一. 小孩子們都喜歡放花。
   二. 這個紅花兒真好看。
2. 聲 shēng BF: sound, voice
   四聲 N: the four tones of the Chinese-Mandarin spoken language
   一. 四聲在中文裏非常重要。
3. 音 yīn BF: sound, voice
   聲音 N: sound, voice
   一. 他說話的聲音很好聽。
4. 讓 ràng V/CV: let, allow/by (governing agent in "passive" constructions)
   一. 請你先讓我過去。
   二. 魚讓孩子們都吃完了。
5. 類 lèi M: class, species, kind
   一. 我們都喜歡念這類的書。
6. 休 syōu BF: rest
7. 息 syí BF: rest
   休息 V/N: rest
   一. 他已經休息了半個鐘頭了。
   二. 我忙的連一分鐘的休息都沒有。
8. 式 shr̀ BF: form, fashion, style
   中式(的) N: Chinese style
   正式(的) A: formally
   非正式(的) A: informally
   一. 這張 桌子是中式的，不是西式的。
   二. 他跟我非正式的談過一次。
9. 燈 dēng N: lantern, lamp

花燈 N: colored lantern

點燈 VO: light a lamp

一. 王小姐作的花燈最好看。

二. 他不喜歡點着燈睡覺。

10. 普 pǔ BF: universal, general

11. 通 tūng BF: universal; [go through]

普通 SV: be common, in general use

一. 這是一句很普通的話。

12. 馬 mǎ N: horse

走馬燈 N: a lantern with a circle of paper cutouts of horses (or other animals) mounted around the candle so that the ascending hot air will cause them to revolve

13. 電 dyàn N: electricity

電燈 N: electric light

一. 今天晚上没電,各家的電燈都不亮。

14. 收 shōu V: put away; [receive; collect]

收起來 V: put away

一. 快點兒把這些東西收起來。

15. 春 chwūn BF: spring (season)

春天 TW: springtime

一. 到了春天，各種花兒就都開了。

Marble Boat, Summer Palace
Peking

Notes

1. 放花-pàu (-炮) VO: let off fireworks
   放花 VO: let off fireworks other than fire-crackers
   放-pàu (-炮) VO: let off fire-crackers
2. 信 V: believe, believe in
   信-gwěi (-鬼) VO: believe in ghosts
   一. 你不信我，我就不能再幫忙了。
   二. 我聽說有很多人信 gwěi。
3. 不可少 SV: be indispensable
   一. 有人說，錢是不可少的東西。
4. 大多數 N: the great majority
   一. 美國人大多數喜歡吃魚。
5. tyē (貼) V: paste, stick on
6. "一-rù (入) 新年, fú (福) 在 yǎn (眼)-前" Ph: "As you enter the new year, blessings await you"—a very common new-year motto
7. 燈-jyé (-節) N: the Lantern Festival (which falls on the 15th day of the first lunar month)
8. gwà (掛) V: hang
9. dùngwù (動物) N: animal
10. jwàn-來-jwàn-去 (轉) V: revolve on and on—when this pattern is used with other verbs of movement like 跑來跑去，走來走去 etc., it means "back and forth"
11. 人山人海 Ph: a huge crowd—lit. human mountain, human sea

12. 吃喝玩兒-lè(-樂) Ph: feasting, having a good time--lit. eat, drink, play and rejoice
13. 工作 V/N: work
14. 謝天謝地 IE: thank heavens—lit. thank heaven, thank earth
15. gwēigwei ijyujyū-的 A: regularly, back to norm
(規規矩矩)

View of Tien An Men Square

第七課　五月-jyé 跟八月-jyé

在紀-ywàn前第四世紀的時候，Chǔ-國—就是現在的湖北湖南一帶—有一位最有名的shr̄-人。他因爲Chǔ-王不用他，於是就跳在江裏自殺了。Chǔ-國的人很túng-情他，就坐船到處找他的shr̄shǒu. 後來變成了一個全國的風俗：每年在陰-lì五月chū-五他死的那一天紀念他。這就是現在的五月-jyé.

現在五月-jyé這天，全國的人都吃dzùng子。包dzùng-子的法子是用júyè包上米。有時候還有別的東西，放在水裏jǔ-了吃。南方水多的地方還在這天sài lúng-船，非常熱鬧。現在每年過五月-jyè的人是不是心裏還都紀念這位shr̄-人，沒法子說。可是五月-jyé沒有問題的是中國三大jyé裏的一個大jyé.

除了年-jyé跟五月-jyé以外，中國第三個大jyé是在陰-lì八月十五這天過的八月-jyé. 這時候是陽-lì九月或是十月，已經是秋天了。Núng-人一年的工作都忙完了，天氣也慢慢的涼快了。在這個時候應當有一個jyé，叫人快-le快-le，休息休息。這也許是八月-jyé爲甚麽是一個大jyé的原故吧。

下面這個故事是不是真的不要緊，談起來非常有意思。陰-lì八月十五，月亮正是最圓的時候。中國人看月亮上黑的地方像一個 tù-兒。於是傳說月亮裏住着一個 tù-兒,會作長生不老的yàu.每年在八月 jyé 這一天，很多人都拜 tù-兒-yé,說那天是他的生日。

八月-jyé 的時候，街上除了有很多賣 tú-兒-yé 的地方以外,還有很多賣月-bǐng 的地方。本來月-bǐng 是爲jì tù-兒 yé用的。現在當然很多人買月-bǐng 就是爲自已吃，因爲差不多没人不愛吃月-bǐng.

我們在這三課裏講的只是中國的三個大 jyé. 另外還有一些jyé,也都是很有意思的。因爲一個一個的講起來太長，佔的地方太多，所以只好暫且不談了。

中國雖然已經改用陽-lì 了，可是中國現在還過這些jyé,因爲這些jyé 早就變成了中國生活的一部分了。

(一) 黃先生早上打了一個電話，讓我把一切都預備好。十五號他一來，我們就一塊兒到上海去。

(二) 據說那個地方樹木很多，可是地方總是不大乾淨。

(三) 你在風裏站得太久了，恐怕就要着涼了。

(四) 他因爲殺了一個人，自己也跳海自殺了。

(五) 這個海口沒問題的是北部的商業中心。

(六) 我忘了全世界一共有幾個大洋了。可是我準知道有太平洋跟大西洋。

(七) 現代的發明一天比一天多。人類的進步真是快極了。

(八) 造紙是中國發明的。

Vocabulary

1. 跳 tyàu V: jump
   跳海 VO: jump into the sea (to end one's life)
   一. 他跳得很高。
   二. 他覺得活着沒意思，就跳了海了。
2. 殺 shā V: kill
   自殺 V: commit suicide
   一. 他殺了那個人以後就自殺了。
3. 處 chù BF: place
   到處，各處，四處，處處 N: everywhere
   一. 過年的時候到處都看得見花燈。
4. 風 fēng N/BF: wind/custom
   一. 今天的風很大。
5. 俗 sú BF/SV: be common ; [vulgar]
   風俗 N: custom
   一. 中國有很多有意思的風俗。
6. 死 sž V: die, be dead
   一. 他父親死了。

7. 包 bāu V/M: wrap/parcel, pack, package
包起來 or 包上 RV: wrap up
一. 請你把這兩包點心包起來。

8. 米 mǐ N: hulled rice, grain, uncooked rice

9. 題 tí BF: theme, subject
問題 N: question, problem
沒(有)問題的 A: unquestionably
一. 我沒(有)問題的可以幫你的忙。

10. 或 hwò BF: either, or
或是 MA: either, or
一. 或是你去或是他去都可以。

11. 秋 chyōu BF: autumn
秋天 TW: autumn
一. 這兒的秋天很涼快。

12. 涼 lyáng SV: be cool, cold
涼快 SV: be cool
着涼 VO: catch cold (着 is pronounced jāu here)
一. 這兒的水太涼。
二. 白天熱，晚上涼快。
三. 他昨天着涼了，今天還沒好呢。

13. 圓 ywán SV: be round, circular
一. 今天晚上的月亮很圓。

14. 另 lìng Sp: another, besides, in addition
另外 Sp/MA: another/besides, in addition
一. 你說的是另一件事。
二. 另外一個人今天不能來。
三. (另外)請你(另外)作一個句子。

15. 改 gǎi V: alter, change
一. 這件衣-shang 請你給我改一改。

Notes

1.	五月 -jyé (-節)	N:	the Dragon-Boat Festival on the 5th day of the 5th lunar month
	八月 -jyé (-節)	N:	the Mid-Autumn Festival on the 15th day of the 8th lunar month
2.	Chǔ-國 (楚-)	PW:	the state of Chu, one of the powerful feudal states which existed from 740 to 330 B.C.
	Chǔ-王 (楚-)	N:	the king of Chu
3.	湖北	PW:	Hupeh province (in central China)
	湖南	PW:	Hunan province (in central China)
4.	shr̄-人 (詩-)	N:	poet — from shr̄ (poetry, ode) and 人
5.	於是	MA:	then, thereupon
6.	túng-情 (同-)	V:	sympathize (share the feelings) — a VO more often used as a V
7.	shr̄shǒu (尸首)	N:	corpse
8.	紀念	V/N:	commemorate/commemoration, memorial, something to remember by — from 紀 (remember — interchangeable with 記 in this sense) and 念 (think of) 一. 我們都要紀念這一天。 二. 這是一個很好的紀念。

9. dzùng-子 (粽-) N: a certain kind of dumplings made by wrapping glutinous rice or millet in broad bamboo leaves, usually in the shape of a tetrahedron, and boiling them

10. júyè (竹葉) N: bamboo leaves—from jú (bamboo) and yè (leaf)

11. jǔ (煮) V: boil

12. sài lúng-船 (賽龍-) VO: race the dragon-boats—from sài (compete), lúng (dragon) and 船 (boat)

13. 年-jyé (-節) N: New Year Festival

14. núng-人 (農-) N: farmer—from núng (agriculture) and 人

15. 快-lè (-樂) V/SV/N: rejoice/be happy/joy

16. 月亮 N: the moon

17. tù-兒 (兔-) N: rabbit, hare

Tù-兒-yé (兔兒爺) N: a hare which is supposed to dwell in the moon and assist in preparing the elixir of immortality

18. 傳說 V/N: it is said/hearsay, transmit by tradition

一. 傳說你要到日本去，是真的嗎？

二. 那只是一種傳說，我不會去的。

19. 長生不老 IE: immortality—lit. long life without old (age)

一. 人要是能長生不老多麽好！

20. 生日 N: birthday

21. 月-bǐng (-餅) N: moon-cake, a round-shaped cake, usually stuffed with sweet edibles and eaten at the Mid-Autumn Festival—

bǐng is pronounced with a low tone when stressed

22. 樹木 N: trees

23. 現代 N: the present generation, the present time

一. 張先生是現代一位有名的人。

24. 人類 N: mankind

一. 人類的生活一天比一天進步。

West Lake (Syī Hú)
Jèjiāng province.

第八課　中國俗話（一）

每一個民dzú都有他們自己常說的俗話。這些俗話都是用不多的字就把一個道理或是一個理想說得很清楚，叫人很容易記住。俗話多半都是父親傳給兒子，兒子再傳給他的兒子，這樣一代一代的傳留下來的，沒有作jě. 中國已經有了三四千年的lìshř，傳留下來很多的俗話。我們在這一課跟下一課裏要介紹幾句最普通的中國俗話。

有一些俗話是告訴人怎麼做人這一類的話，可以說都是géyán. 比方說，有一句俗話是：「話到口邊留半句，得ráu人處且ráu人。」意思是在你生氣的時候，別把你心裏想說的話都說出來。你要是把你生氣的話都說出來，後來一定會後hwěi. 所以在這時候應當把要說的話留一半，能讓人的地方總要讓人。

還有一句俗話是：「打人別打臉，mà人別mà短。」當然人都不應當打人或是mà人。可是你要是自己管不住自己，必得打人或是mà人的時候，最好別打人的臉或是mà人的短處，因爲那都是讓人最生氣的事情。

關於勸人別作不好的事情也有一句俗話：「白天

不作kwēi-心事，半夜不怕gwěi叫門。」人要是沒作甚麽壞事，心裏當然很平安。心裏很平安，還怕半夜有gwěi來叫門嗎？

「救人救到底，送人送到家」也是常說的一句俗話。意思是不管作甚麽事，總要有shř有jūng.起-shř-了一件事，就應當把那件事作完了，別作到一半就不作了。

有一句俗話勸人應當愛-syī時間。這句俗話是:「一寸光陰一寸金，寸金難買寸光陰。」「一寸長的光陰好像一寸長的金子那麽jŕ-錢。可是用一寸長的金子也很難買一寸長的光陰。所以人人都應當愛-syī光陰，不應當làngfèi時間。

（一）外面整天整夜用車運很重的石頭，聲音大極了。白天作了一天事，晚上連休息都不能休息。

（二）還沒到秋天呢，包太太就把他改的那件皮大衣穿上了。

（三）你跟我一塊兒去接他好不好？我可以給你們介紹介紹。

（四）他不但愛畫畫兒，並且也愛念書。

Vocabulary

1. 理 lǐ BF: principle
   道理 N: principles, the rightness of things
   理想 SV/N: ideal
   一. 你這麼作很有道理。
   二. 在這個地方念書很理想。
   三. 他的理想很高。
2. 清 chīng BF: be clear, pure
3. 楚 chǔ BF/N: be clear/(a surname), (name of an ancient state)
   清楚 SV: be clear
   一. 請你說清楚一點兒，我聽不懂。
4. 記 jì V: remember, recollect
   記住 RV: fix in mind
   記得 V: remember
   一. 我的記-syìng不好，記不住今天念的生字。
   二. 我記得我在日本見過他。
5. 留 lyóu V: keep; [preserve]
   傳留 V: hand down
   一. 我想留你在我家住幾天。
   二. 風俗都是傳留下來的。
6. 介 jyè BF: lie between
7. 紹 shàu BF: connect, join
   介紹 V: introduce (lit. to serve as an intermediary)
   一. 請你給我介紹一個女朋友。
8. 管 gwǎn V: control, manage, attend to
   不管 V: don't care whether, no matter whether

一. 他的事你別管。

二. 你愛怎麽作就怎麽作，我管不着。

三. 不管誰去都成,可是必得有一個去。

9. 勸 chywàn V: exhort, advise, persuade

一. 我勸你別常喝酒。

10. 安 ān BF: peace

平安 SV/N: be peaceful /peace

一. 母親的信上說他們很平安。

二. 忘了自己，心裏就有了平安了。

11. 救 jyòu V: save, rescue

一. 有一句俗話說,救別人就是救自己。

12. 間 jyān BF/M: among, the space between/(for rooms)

時間 N: time, period

一. 時間不早了，我應當走了。

二. 我家有七間屋子。

13. 寸 tswùn M: an inch

一. 這張紙有十寸長。

14. 光 gwāng N: light, brightness

光陰 N: time (lit. light and shade)

一. 太陽的光很亮。

二. 光陰過的真快。

15. 金 jīn BF: gold

金子 N: gold

舊金山 PW: San Francisco (named from the Gold Rush)

一. 舊金山從前出金子,所以叫舊金山。

Notes

1.	俗話	N:	common saying, proverb
2.	民 -dzú (-族)	N:	race; nation (in the sense of the people)—from 民 (people) and dzú (tribe)
3.	一代一代的	Ph:	generation by generation 一. 俗話都是一代一代的傳下來的。
4.	作 -jě (-者)	N:	writer, author—from 作 (write) and jě (one who, those who)
5.	做人	VO:	(the way one) acts as a person
6.	géyán 格言	N:	motto, maxim
7.	"話到口邊留半句，得 ráu 人處且 ráu 人。"	Ph:	"Don't say everything you feel like saying at the moment; whenever you can forgive, forgive."
	得 (dé)	AV:	can—note the word 得 has been introduced as a particle (read de) and as an auxiliary verb (read děi)
	ráu (饒)	V:	forgive
	且	A:	under the circumstances—note its new meaning in addition to "moreover"
8.	後 -hwěi (悔)	V:	regret—from 後 (afterwards) and hwěi (regret)
9.	讓	V:	yield (to others)—note the new meaning of 讓 一. 你比他大，讓他一點兒好不好？
10.	"打人別打臉，mà 人別 mà 短。"	Ph:	"When you hit somebody, don't hit his face; when you scold somebody, don't scold him over his shortcomings."
	mà (罵)	V:	scold, curse

11.	短處	N:	shortcoming
12.	"白天不作 kwēi-心事，半夜不怕 gwěi 叫門。"	Ph:	"Do nothing discreditable during the day, be unafraid of any ghost that may come to knock on the door at midnight."
	kwēi-心事 (虧-)	N:	a discreditable behavior—from <u>kwēi</u> (deficient), 心(heart) and 事(affair)
13.	"救人救到底，送人送到家。"	Ph:	"If you save a man, save him thoroughly; if you see a person home, see him all the way to his home."
14.	有 shř (始) 有 jūng (終)	Ph:	finish what one started (lit. having a beginning and an end)
15.	起 -shř (-始)	V:	begin
16.	愛 -syī (-惜)	V:	love and care
17.	"一寸光陰一寸金，寸金難買寸光陰。"	Ph:	"An inch of time, an inch of gold; and an inch of gold cannot buy an inch of time."
18.	làngfèi (浪費)	V:	waste
19.	皮大衣	N:	fur-coat

Gate of Summer Palace

第九課 中國俗話（二）

還有一種俗話，說的都是人的經-yàn.「不怕慢，只怕站」的意思很清楚。無論作甚麼事，慢一點兒沒甚麼關-syi, 可是千萬別停住不作了。慢一點兒有作完了的時候，學會了的時候。要是停住不作下去，就沒有作完了，學會了的希望了。

有一句俗話勸人說話要小心，別隨便說話。這句俗話是:「走錯了路回得來，說錯了話回不來。」走錯了路可以回來再走。說錯了話已經叫聽見的人不高-syìng-了，後-hwěi 也沒用了。所以最好的法子是說話的時候要小心。

人生活在世界上，最重要的一件事是合作。一個人的力量是小的,大家合起來的力量是大的。西方有一句俗話說:「兩個人的頭-nǎu比一個人的好。」中國也有這麼一句俗話，就是:「二人同心，黃土變金。」作事的時候要是能大家一條心，連黃土都會變成金子的。

人平常總是喜歡買便-yi東西。覺得錢少就上算，錢多就上當。可是很多人不知道便-yi東西也許只用了幾天就壞了。貴一點兒的東西雖然錢多一倍或是兩倍，可是也許用了很久還沒壞呢。所以有一句俗話說:「貴的不貴, 賤的不賤。」意思是貴東西並不一定貴, 賤東西並不一定賤。

人在剛有一點兒學問的時候, 很容易覺得自己已經知道的很多了。Chíshŕ,他所知道的也許才是學問的海裏的一-dī水。所以西方一句俗話說:「有一點兒學問是很危險的事情。」中國也有這樣一句俗話, 可是不直接的說「有一點兒學問很危險;」只是間接的說學問是多麽多, 人一直學到老也學不完。這句俗話是:「活到老, 學到老, 還有三分學不到。」說話的方法不一樣, 可是意思一樣。

要是把中國俗話都寫出來, 一定可以寫很厚的一本書。我們在這兩課裏只說了十句。希望各位dújě學會了這十句以後, 對於中國俗話能有一個大概的gwān-念。

(一) 春天花兒開的時候, 有紅的, 有黄的, 有白的, 好看極了。

(二) 這個地方**越**來**越**熱鬧。

(三) 這封信我不敢說他甚麽時候能收到。你要是叫人特別送去, 那就沒問題的可以收到了。

(四) 他家也沒有電燈, 也沒有電話。我想恐怕是因爲路還沒有通到他們那個地方的原故吧。

(五) 花兒不能總是開着；月亮不能總是圓的；朋友們也不能總是在一塊兒。

(六) 除了這個以外，我都非常喜歡。

(七) 馬先生買了一所兒西式房子。

(八) 洋比海大；海又比湖大。

(九) 他在念書方面很好，可是在作事方面不太好。

Yangtse River Bridge, Nanking

Vocabulary

1. 無 wú BF: without, have not
2. 論 lwùn BF: discuss, argue
   - 無論 or 不論 A: no matter what, it doesn't matter (interchangeable with 不管)
     - 一. 無論你到那兒去，我都跟着你。
3. 停 tíng V: stop
   - 停住 RV: come to a stop, cease
   - 停車 VO: park a car
     - 一. 我的表停了。
     - 二. 請你停住，別說了，我不願意聽。
     - 三. 這個地方可以停車嗎？
4. 隨 swéi BF: follow
   - 隨便 SV/A: do as one pleases (lit. follow convenience)
     - 一. 這個人說話很隨便。
     - 二. 請你隨便給我們說幾句話。
5. 合 hé V: join
   - 合作 V/N: cooperate/cooperation
     - 一. 我們兩個人的，合起來才有一毛五。
     - 二. 他們不願意跟我們合作。
6. 力 lì BF: strength, power
7. 量 lyàng/lyáng BF/V: capacity/measure
   - 力量 N: strength, vigor (pronounced <u>lìlyang</u>)
   - 商量 V: discuss, talk over (pronounced shāng-lyang)
8. 土 tǔ N: dirt, soil
9. 倍 bèi M: times, -fold
   - 一. 一百是十的十倍。
10. 賤 jyàn SV: be cheap, inexpensive
    - 一. 這個地方裏的東西很賤。

11. 剛 gāng A: just now
 剛才 MA: just a moment ago
 一. 他們剛來。
 二. 剛才我去找你，你没在家。
12. 危 wéi, wēi BF: be dangerous, perilous
13. 險 syǎn BF: be dangerous, perilous
 危險 SV/N: be dangerous, perilous/danger
 一. 這條路很危險。
 二. 現在這帶地方没有甚麽危險。
14. 厚 hòu SV: be thick
 一. 這張紙很厚。
15. 概 gài BF: in general
 大概 MA: probably
 一. 他們大概都走了。

Notes

1. 經-yàn (-驗) N: experience
2. "不怕慢，只怕站。" Ph: "Fear not being slow; fear standing still."
3. 關-syi (-係) N: relation, relationship, relevance — 係 is pronounced with falling tone, syì, when stressed
4. "走錯了路回得來，說錯了話回不來。" Ph: "If you go the wrong road, you can come back; if you say the wrong words, you can't take them back."
5. 頭-nǎu (-腦) N: head (in the sense of mind) — the

		English proverb referred to is: "Two heads are better than one."
6. "二人 túng-心, 黃土變金"	Ph:	"When two people are of the same mind, even yellow dirt can be changed into gold."
túng-心 (同-)	SV:	be of the same mind
一條心	IE:	of one mind—note the unusual measure for "heart"
7. 上算	SV:	a good bargain
上當	SV:	be swindled, be taken in (note 當 is pronounced dàng here)
		一. 兩塊錢一本很上算。
8. "貴的不貴,賤的不賤。"	Ph:	"The expensive is not expensive; the cheap is not cheap."
9. chíshŕ (其實)	MA:	actually, as a matter of fact
10. dī (滴)	M:	a drop
11. "有一點兒學問是很危險的事情。"	Ph:	"A little learning is a dangerous thing; (Drink deep, or taste not the Pierian spring.)" —from Alexander Pope
12. 直接	A:	directly
間接	A:	indirectly
		一. 請直接到學校去。
		二. 我已經間接的告訴他了。
13. "活到老,學到老,還有三分學不到。"	Ph:	"Live to old age, learn to old age; there are still three-tenths you haven't learned."
三分	N:	three of ten parts
14. dújě (讀者)	N:	the reader, one who reads this
15. gwān-念 (觀-)	N:	concept

第十課　姓名問題

研究中國文-hwà的外國朋友們總覺得中國人的姓名是一個很máfan-的問題。這個問題也許不太máfan, 可是也實在不太簡單。希望各位知道了中國姓名的背景以後，jr̀-少同意中國姓名這麽不簡單是有原故的。

中國雖然人口有八萬萬，可是一共只有四百多個姓。平-jyūn-起來，每一個姓裏同姓的差不多有二百多萬人。多數的中國姓都是一個字的。最普通的是張王李Jàu這些姓。有些姓是兩個字的。姓代表一個家-dzú, 所以無論是在說的時候或是寫的時候，姓總是放在名子前頭，不像美國人總是把姓放在後頭。

中國姓這麽少，怎麽能說máfan呢？Máfan-的部分是姓底下的名子。中國人從一生下來就有一個小名兒。小孩子還在吃nǎi的時候，就給他起這麽一個名子，所以又叫nǎi-名兒。這種名子多半是父母隨便起的一個很親熱的名子，像Bǎubǎu, 小妹這一類的。同時，父母還給起一個正式的名子，常是代表一個理想，希望孩子們後來能實現這個理想。這種正式的名子平常都是兩個字，像Jènhwá, Ywèdzǔ

這類好聽的名子。有時候是一個字，也都是選一些意思很好的字。

所以，中國人的姓名可以少到兩個字，可以多到四個字。大多數人的姓名都是三個字。

女人在結婚以後，就把jàng-夫的姓放在自己姓名的前頭。我們一看見張李歌春這姓名，就知道這位原來是李歌春小姐，現在是一位張先生的太太。這位歌春小姐要是nyáng-家姓Ōu-陽，跟一位Jūgě先生結婚，那麽她的姓名就變成了Jūgě Ōu-陽歌春六個字。不過，姓名有六個字是太不常見的事情。

（一）預備好了這個菜以後，就別再另外預備甚麽了。

（二）談到風景，那大概得算西湖最好一特別是在春天跟秋天一不但樹木多，並且還涼快。

（三）這一帶現在的商業不很好。我準知道這只是暫時的，不久一切就都變好了。

（四）你還記得不記得造紙是在第幾世紀發明的？

（五）據他講，一月一號並不是新年。正月chū-一才是新年呢。

（六）我看見他很快的往前跑了幾步，就跳到河裏去了。恐怕人活着一没意思就可能自殺。

(七) 你别管了。我準全給你洗乾淨,不留到明天。

(八) 他剛離婚了不到一年，就又結婚了。

(九) 對不起，我没工夫。我得在家wēn-習gūng-課。

(十) 長江一帶是出米的地方。

(土) 這個大樹死了，樹皮都没有了。

Vocabulary

1. 研 yán — BF: investigate, research
2. 究 jyōu — BF: examine into

    研究 V/N: research, study (pronounced yánjyou)

    講究 SV: be meticulous; "classy" (pronounced jyǎng-jyou)

    一. 我在這個學校研究中文。

    二. 這是他這五年的研究。

    三. 李太太的皮大衣真講究。

3. 實 shŕ — BF: real, true; [solid]

    實在 A: really, truly

    實現 V: realize (a hope, plan, etc.)

    一. 我實在不願意念書。

    二. 這個理想很難實現。

4. 簡 jyǎn — BF: simple, concise

簡直(的) A: simply; come to the point

一. 他說的話我簡直(的)不懂。

二. 我簡直(的)不知道他是甚麽意思。

5. 單 dān — BF: simple, singly

簡單 SV: be simple (as opposed to complex)

一. 這件事不像你說的那麽簡單。

6. 背 bèi — V/BF: recite/back, behind

背書 VO: repeat a lesson from memory

一. 你把這課書背給我聽。

二. 這本書我全會背。

7. 景 jǐng — BF: view; circumstances

背景 N: background

風景 N: landscape

一. 我不大知道他的背景。

8. 同 túng — BF: be the same

同意 V: agree

同姓的 N: people of the same family name

同時 MA: at the same time

一. 我同意你說的話。

二. 我們三個人同時到的。

9. 李 lǐ — N: (a surname)

行李 N: baggage

一. 李先生就帶了一件大行李。

10. 妹 mèi — BF: younger sister

妹妹 N: younger sister

11. 選 sywǎn — V: choose

一. 他選了半天，可是沒買。

12. 結 jyé — BF: unite, knot

13. 婚 hwūn BF：marriage
結婚 VO: get married, marriage
離婚 VO: divorce
一. 他們剛結婚一年就離婚了。

14. 姐 jyě BF: older sister
姐姐 N: older sister
小姐 N: Miss; daughter (term for some one else's)

15. 習 syí BF: practice, study

Notes

1. 姓名 N: surname and personal name
2. jr̀-少 (至-) A: at least
3. 平-jyūn (-均) A: on the average
4. 家-dzú (-族) N: family clan
5. 一生下來 Ph: since birth, as soon as born
一. 小孩子一生下來就哭。
6. 小名兒 N: pet name given to a child
一. 中國人差不多每一個人都有一個小名兒。
7. nǎi (奶) N: milk
nǎi-名兒 N: pet name given to a child (interchangeable with 小名兒)
8. 起名子 VO: give a name
一. 你的名子是誰給你起的？
9. 親熱 SV: be intimate
一. 他們兩個人親熱極了。

10. Báubau (寶寶) N: (a very common pet name for children)—寶 (bǎu) means precious
11. 小妹 N: Little Sis. (a very common pet name for girls)
12. Jènhwá (振華) N: (a typical Chinese given name, meaning "to uplift China")
13. Ywèdzǔ (耀祖) N: (another typical Chinese given name, meaning "to glorify one's ancestors")
14. 少到…… Ph: as little as ……, as few as ……
多到…… Ph: as many as ……, as much as ……
15. jàng-夫 (丈-) N: husband (more accepted among educated people than the colloquial expression 先生)
16. nyáng-家 (娘-) N: a wife's family
17. Ōu-陽 (歐-) N: (a double surname)
18. Jūgě (諸葛) N: (another double surname)
19. 傳教 VO: preach religion, do missionary work
一. 聽說他到日本傳教去了。
20. wēn-習 (温-) V: review (pronounced wēnsyi)
一. 我們一個禮拜wēn-習一次gūng-課。

The Great Wall

第十一課　再談姓名問題

中國人成人以後，就在名子以外，另外再加上一個字。朋友們就不再叫他的名子，專用他的字來稱-hu他。有時候一個人在字以外，還有號。字跟號都是自己起的，或是旁人送的。要不是代表自己的理想，就是代表自己的愛好。因爲一個人的理想跟愛好有時候改變，所以有時候一個人有好幾個號。中國大畫家Chí白石有兩個字：一個是自己起的，一個是dzǔ父給他起的。他有一個號。在這個號以外，還有十三個別號。最常用的一個是白石老人。

有名的人，在名，字跟號以外，還常有旁的名稱。別人因爲要dzwūnjìng他，就常用他生的地方，或是住的地方的名子，他的書房或是花-ywán-的名子，或是他的官-jŕ來稱-hu他。Chīnglyán Jyūshr̀，隨-ywán先生，Dù-工部，都是這一類的名稱。

最後，我們談談外國人怎麽起中國名子。外國人起中國名子，普通用兩種方法。一種是按着他本國名子的聲音起一個中國名子。選的幾個字放在一塊兒，没有甚麽意思，只是他本國名子的聲音。如同華-shèngdwùn這類的名子，一聽就知道是外國人的名子。另外一種方法是按着起中國姓名的方法起一個中國姓名。如同Láng 世 -níng 這類的姓名，聽着看着都完全跟中國姓名一樣。

按着中國這個老方法,一個人有這麽多名稱,爲旁人們實在不方便。特別是記性不好的人，簡直的是記不住。所以現在很多人都是「名號一-jr̀」。意思是名就是號，號就是名。一個人只有一個名子。有些中國人到外國去,還用他們的中國名子,不改成Bǐ- 得或是保 -lwó 也是因爲這個原故。

(一) 我没力量救你。我介紹你去找他幫你的忙吧。

(二) 我買的一整包洋火，全讓他拿走了，一包也没留。

(三) 連一寸光陰都是好的。所以人都應當愛 -syī 光陰。

(四) 這些日子我的運氣不好，並且天氣也太熱，所以我暫且要休息幾天。

(五) 世界各處現在没有一個真正平安的地方。

(六) 世界各處的人民向來最愛自 -yóu 。

(七) 你除了别跟我借錢以外，甚麽都行。

(八) 我是鄉下人，不懂甚麽規 -jyu。

Vocabulary

1. 加 jyā　V: add, increase
   一. 你的車要加水嗎？
   二. 原來只有兩個人去，現在又加上一個。
2. 專 jwān　A: solely, specially
   一. 我上街沒別的事,專給你買東西。
3. 稱 chēng　V: call (in the sense of addressing by a specified name)
   名稱　N: name, appellation
4. 旁 páng　BF: other; by the side of
   旁人　N: other people, a bystander
   一. 旁人的事最好少管。
5. 官 gwān　N: official, officer
   一. 他父親是一個大官。
6. 按 àn　CV: according to
   一. 我們都要按(着)他的意思作。
7. 如 rú　BF: be like, as
   如同　A: resemble, be like
   一. 到了舊金山的中國城就如同到了中國一樣。
8. 華 hwá　BF: glory, splendor
   中華民國　PW: The Republic of China
   一. 一九五六年是中華民國四十五年。
9. 性 syìng　BF: nature, disposition
   記性　N: memory
10. 保 bǎu　BF: protect, guarantee
11. 主 jǔ　BF: master; main, chief
   主意　N: idea, plan—note 主 is pronounced

jú here

民主 SV: be democratic

一. 你這個主意真好。

二. 在一個民主國家裏甚麽都應當很民主。

12. 向 syàng BF: hitherto

向來 MA: hitherto, habitually

一. 你聽誰說我喝酒？我向來不喝。

13. 借 jyè V: lend; borrow

借給 V: lend

一. 可以借給人錢，可是別跟人借錢。

14. 鄉 syāng BF: the country (as contrasted with the town)

鄉下 PW: the country, rural district

一. 美國有很多人喜歡在鄉下住。

15. 規 gwēi BF: rule, regulation (lit. compasses)

規-jyu N: rules and regulations

Notes

1. 成人 N/VO: an adult/become a man

一. 成人跟孩子都可以進來。

二. 成(了)人以後就不應當哭了。

2. 字 N: courtesy name (formerly taken at the age of twenty)

一. 他姓高，叫華春，字是向前。

3. 稱-hu (-呼) V: call (one's name)

4.	號	N:	fancy name of a person
5.	愛好	N:	what one is fond of—好 is pronounced hàu here
6.	改變	V/N:	change 一. 他回來以後改變了很多。 二. 這一次的改變很大。
7.	畫家	N:	artist, painter
8.	Chí白石（齊）	N:	Ch'i Pai-shih, probably the most famous contemporary Chinese painter
9.	dzǔ-父（祖-）	N:	paternal grandfather
10.	別號	N:	a person's fancy name by which he is generally known, an alias
11.	dzwūnjìng（尊敬）	V:	respect
12.	花-ywán（-園）	N:	a flower-garden
13.	官-jŕ（-職）	N:	official title or rank
14.	Chīnglyán Jyūshr̀（青蓮居士）	N:	Retired Scholar of the Green Lotus (lit. Green-Lotus Retired-Scholar), a fancy name given to Lǐ Bái (Li Po, 李白), one of the two most celebrated poets of the T'ang Dynasty, who was born in the Green Lotus Village in Sz̀chwān (Szechwan) province
15.	隨-ywán 先生(-園)	N:	Gentleman of the Let-It-Be Garden, an alias given to Ywán Méi (袁枚), a famous scholar-official of the Ching Dynasty
16.	Dù 工部（杜）	N:	an alias given to Dù Fǔ (Tu Fu, 杜甫), the other one of the two most

celebrated poets of the T'ang Dynasty, due to the fact that he served as a second-secretary in the Board of Works (工部)

17. 華-shèngdwùn(-盛頓) N: (transliteration of) Washington

18. Láng 世-níng (郎世寧) N: Joseph Castilhoni, an Italian painter who, during the reign of Chyánlúng (Ch'ien-lung), served in the Chinese royal palace and started a mixed style of Chinese and Western paintings

19. "名號一-jr̀"(-致) Ph: having only one name (lit. name and fancy name the same)

20. Bǐ-得 (彼-) N: (transliteration of) Peter—得 is pronounced dé here

21. 保-lwó (-羅) N: (transliteration of) Paul

22. 真正 A: really, genuinely

第十二課　家-dzú觀念

在美國常說的一種笑話是關於ywè-母跟pwó-母的笑話。這種笑話在中國的社會裏很少聽見，因爲中美兩國的家-tíng jr̀-度不一樣。在美國的小家-tíng-裏，ywè-母pwó-母不跟兒子女兒住在一塊兒。他們到兒子女兒家去　要是住的太久，或是喜歡多說話，就要鬧笑話。在中國原來的大家-tíng-裏，pwó-母是家-tíng-裏的一部分。Ywè-母到女兒家去是客人，最多住幾天，也不多說話，管女兒家的事。所以没有這類的笑話。

中國的大家-tíng jr̀-度的一個最重要的理論是：一個人不是一個自由的個人，而是家-dzú-的一部分。他最大的dzérèn是jìsyù他這個家-dzú-的生命。所以有一句話說:「不syàu有三，無後爲大」。西方國家說家-pǔ是一-kē樹，恐怕也是這意思。不過，中國特別注重這個意思。每一個人都是他那個家-dzú-的樹上的一個jr̄-子。這-kē大樹由他這個jr̄-子再jìsyù-的生長發展。這是他對於他的家-dzú的dzérèn.

因爲這個原故，結婚這件事就變成了家-tíng的事了。父母要替兒子選一個合-shr̀-的家-tíng-的女孩子。兒子願意不願意是小事，兩家一定要「門當hù對」是大事。因爲結婚不是自己的事，而是要永遠的jìsyù家-dzú-的生命。

由這種家-dzú觀念裏產生出來一個人生jé-學,就是：人活着要不給祖先丢人，並且要給他們這一姓生幾個好兒子，讓祖先覺得體面。由這種家-dzú觀念，這種人生jé學，又產生出來拜祖先的風俗來。在過年過jyé的時候要拜祖先。有人說，這不只是一種風俗，而是一種宗教。這麽講也不能說没理。Jr̀-少,拜祖先這件事是中國幾個宗教的jīchǔ.

中國這幾十年,各方面很shòu西洋的yǐng-syǎng.家-tíng jr̀-度也不是一個lì-外。小家-tíng jr̀-度越來越普通；大家-tíng jr̀-度越來越不-shòu歡迎。中國懂ywè-母的笑話的也越來越多。

（一）這個電燈非常亮，比平常的亮好幾倍。

（二）開車的時候，看見紅燈就一定得停。要是没看清楚，没停，那就很危險了。

（三）他的臉皮真厚！我勸你別請他。

（四）美國西部的土黃得像金子一樣。據說，土裏真有金子。

（五）請你把我昨天接到的那封信替我收起來。

（六）這個小孩子佔不了多大地方。讓他坐在你們兩個人中間吧。

（七） 李小姐的妹妹性情很特別。

（八） 我不敢在海邊兒上玩兒。

（九） 這個圓屋子裏有很多馬。

（十） 請不必來接我。我明天準來。

（十一） 東西總是**越**來**越**貴，不**越**來**越**賤。

Vocabulary

1. 觀 gwān BF: view, conception, look at
   觀念 N: a concept
   一. 我母親的觀念都太舊了。
2. 社 shè BF: society, community
   社會 N: society
   一. 社會上有各種不同的人。
3. 度 dù BF: a rule, a law; [standard, degree]
4. 由 yóu BF/CV: follow, from/by, through (literary equivalent of 從)
   自由 SV/N: be free/freedom
   一. 這件事由你辦吧。我沒工夫管了。
   二. 他太太回家看母親去了，所以現在他很自由。
   三. 人類都愛自由。
5. 而 ér L: but, while on the other hand, and yet
   不是…而是… Ph: not ……, but ……
   一. 我不是不喜歡跟別人一塊兒去，而是不喜歡跟他一塊兒去。

6. 命 mìng N: life (as opposed to death)

生命 N: life

一. 人的生命比甚麽都重要。

7. 注 jù BF: fix the mind on

注重 V: emphasize

一. 我們都非常注重這件事。

8. 展 jǎn BF: unfold, open

發展 V/N: develop/development

一. 美國的商業發展得很快。

二. 這件事有甚麽新發展嗎？

9. 替 tì CV: for (in place of), substitute for

一. 請放心，這件事我一定替你辦。

10. 永 yǔng BF: perpetual, eternal

永遠 A: always, forever

永遠不 A: never

一. 我永遠愛你。

二. 希望你永遠不離開我。

11. 祖 dzǔ BF: an ancestor

祖先or祖宗 N: ancestors

祖父 N: paternal grandfather

12. 丢 dyōu V: lose

丢人or丢臉VO/SV:"lose face"/be disgraceful

一. 張太太常丢東西。

二. 他不喜歡念書，真給他父親丢人。

三. 你不覺得很丢臉嗎？

13. 體 tǐ BF: the body

體面 SV: be respectable, proud of

一. 他兒子喜歡念書。他覺得很體面。

14. 宗 dzūng BF: ancestor; a school (as of art, religion, etc.)

宗教 N: religion

一. 有人甚麼宗教都不信。

15. 迎 yíng BF: welcome, go to meet

歡迎 V: welcome

一. 昨天我到的時候,他們都來歡迎我。

Notes

1. ywè-母 (岳-) N: wife's mother
2. pwó-母 (婆-) N: husband's mother
3. 家-tíng jr̀dù (家庭制度) N: family system

   小家-tíng jr̀dù N: a system under which a separate home is set up by a young couple

   大家-tíng jr̀dù N: an old system under which family members of two or more generations live together
4. 鬧笑話 VO: make a fool of oneself
5. 理論 N: theory
6. 個人 N: an individual
7. dzérèn (責任) N: responsibility
8. jìsyù (繼續) V/A: continue, carry on/[continuously]
9. "不-syàu有三, 無後爲大" Ph: "There are three things which are unfilial, and to have no posterity is the greatest of them." (the other two being encouraging parents in unrighteousness and not to succor

their poverty and old age by engaging in official service)—a quotation from Mencius

	syàu (孝)	SV: be filial
10.	家-pǔ (-譜)	N: family tree, family register and records
11.	kē (棵)	M: (for trees)
12.	jr̄-子 (枝-)	N: branch, twig
13.	合-shr̀ (-適)	SV: be suitable, fitting
14.	"門當hù對"(戶)	Ph: a suitable marriage—lit. 門 (door), 當 (matching one another), hù (door) and 對 (comparable), referring to families of the same social standing
15.	產生	V: produce, beget (ideology, custom, etc.)
16.	人生jè-學 (哲-)	N: philosophy of life
17.	沒理	VO: be without reason
	有理	VO: have reason —. 他這麽作有理，你不能說他沒理。
18.	jīchǔ (基礎)	N: foundation
19.	shòu…yǐngsyǎng (受…影響)	Ph: influenced by … (lit. receive …… influence)
20.	lì-外 (例-)	N: exception
21.	臉皮	N: skin of the face—usually referred to as being thick (shameless) or thin (bashful)
22.	中間	N: the middle —. 請你坐在我們兩個人中間。
23.	性情	N: disposition —. 他的性情很好。

第十三課　中國的宗教（一）

中國的三大宗教是Kǔng-教，道教跟Fwó-教。Chí-實，Kǔng-教並不是一種宗教；信Kǔng-教的人也不說Kǔng-子是神。Kǔng-子是生在紀-ywán-前第六世紀的一位中國大jé-學家。他的理想是改-shàn人的行爲，改-shàn政府，實現一個理想世界。他雖然沒得到機會實行他改-shàn政府的理想，可是得了很高的代價，因爲他所講的影-syǎng-了中國兩千多年。Kǔng-子一生只是教學生，講學問，沒傳過任何宗教。不但沒傳過教，並且還說過「Wèi知生，yān知死，」「Jìng gwěi神而遠jr」這一類的話。所以Kǔng-教只能算是一種jé學，告訴人怎麽在一塊兒生活。不跟別的宗教一樣，注重信上-dì跟來世這些事情。

道教原來也是一種jé-學。後來才慢慢的變成了宗教。這個jé-學的shř-祖是老子。老子也是紀-ywán-前第六世紀的一位中國大jé-學家。關於他的事情，lìshř-上寫的一點兒也不詳細。結果他變成了一個很神-mì-的人。他的「清淨無爲」的jé-學主張人心裏要清淨，並且政府不要管人民的事情。可惜他只寫了一本五千字的書，用很不容易懂的話講他的jé-學。後來他的jé-學變成了宗教以後，他寫的這本書也變成了道教的根據了。

紀-ywàn-前第六世紀真是人類lìshř-上一個wěi-大的世紀。世界上三位wěi-人，中國三大宗教的shř-祖，都生在這個世紀。生在中國的是剛才講過的Kǔng-子跟老子。生在Yìn-度的是Fwó-教的shř-祖Shr̀jyāmóuní. Fwó-教在差不多兩千年以前從Yìn-度傳到中國來。可以說原來是一個外國宗教。不過，後來加上了很多中國神話風俗等等，使Fwó-教慢慢的變成了一個中國風味很大的宗教。

（一）有一件事情我要跟你商量商量。

（二）希望有一個像你這麼有研究的人替我預備一切。秋天一涼快，大概就可以正式的造了。

（三）湖旁邊兒的地總是不很乾，常有水。有時候得走一步，跳一步，或是在木頭上走才成呢。

（四）三江口那個地方，今年春天出了很多米。

（五）他沒有甚麽黨的背景，也不預備進甚麽黨。

（六）這個花兒不能放在太陽底下。

（七）這件事很簡單，一點兒也不難。

（八）我wēn-習gūng-課wēn-習了整三天。

（九）他父親死了，給他留下很多產業。

Vocabulary

1. 神 shén — N: spiritual being, god
   - 神話 — N: a myth
   - 留神 — VO: take care (= 留心, keep the mind on)
     - 一. 晚上出去的時候要留神。
2. 政 jèng — BF: government, administration
3. 府 fǔ — BF: prefecture; mansion
   - 政府 — N: the government
   - 府上 — IE: home, residence, family (courteous reference to other people's)
     - 一. 府上都好嗎？
4. 機 jī — BF: opportune; [machine]
   - 機會 — N: opportunity
     - 一. 我希望以後有機會去。
5. 價 jyà — BF: price, value
   - 代價 — N: compensation, equivalent price
     - 一. 做事不能沒有代價。
6. 影 yǐng — BF: shadow, reflection
   - 電影兒 — N: motion picture
7. 任 rèn — BF: allow, tolerate—pronounced rén as a surname
8. 何 hé — BF: what? how? why? which?
   - 任何 — N: any
   - 何必 — A: why is it necessary to?
     - 一. 我沒告訴任何人。
     - 二. 你何必一定要去？你不能請他來嗎？
9. 詳 syáng — BF: in detail
10. 細 syì — BF: fine, minute

詳細 SV: be in detail

一. 他的報告很詳細。

11. 果 gwǒ BF: consequence; fruit

結果 N/MA: result, consequence/as a result, consequently

水果 N: fresh fruits

一. 壞人一定有壞結果。

二. 我們都不喜歡吃水果。結果叫他一個人都吃了。

12. 惜 syī BF: to pity

可惜 MA/SV: unfortunately, what a pity!/be pitiful, regrettable

愛惜 V: love and be careful about

一. 我母親最愛我。可惜他已經死了。

二. 他死的很可惜。

三. 中國的老先生常勸人愛惜時間。

13. 根 gēn BF: root, basis

根據 V/N: base on/basis

一. 政府應當根據人民的意思作事。

二. 你說他不好, 有甚麽根據嗎?

14. 使 shř CV: cause—interchangeable with 讓 and 叫 in this sense

一. 這件事使他很丢臉。

15. 味 wèi BF: flavor, taste

風味 N: taste (of a book, etc.), relish

一. 他家裏的東西講究極了, 很有中國風味。

Notes

1. Kŭng-教 (孔-) N: Confucianism—from Kŭng (Confucian) and 教 (religion, teaching)
2. 道教 N: Taoism—from 道 (The Way) and 教 (religion)
3. Fwó-教 (佛-) N: Buddhism—from Fwó (Buddha) and 教 (religion)
4. jé-學家 (哲-) N: philosopher
   jé-學 N: philosophy—from jé (wise) and 學 (learning)
5. 改-shàn (-善) V: better, improve, (lit. change to good)
6. 行爲 N: conduct, behavior—from 行 (do) and 爲 (practice)—note 爲 is pronounced wéi here
   一. 他的行爲不好。你應當小心一點兒。
7. 實行 V: apply, put into practice
   一. 這個意思很不容易實行。
8. 一生 TW: one's whole life
   一. 他一生傳教，講愛人的道理。
9. "Wèi 知生, (未) yān 知死" (焉) Ph: (from the Confucian Analects, the literal translation of which is:) "Not yet know life, how know death?"
10. "Jìng gwěi (敬) (鬼) 神而遠 jr" (之) Ph: "While respecting spiritual beings, keep them at a distance."—from the Confucian Analects
11. 上-dì (-帝) N: God
12. 來世 TW: next life
    一. 現在作好人，來世一定有好結果。

13. shř-祖 (始-) N: founder, first ancestor

14. 老子 N: Laotse, traditionally dated in the 6th century B.C., but now believed to be much later, founder of Taoism and one of the greatest Chinese philosophers—note 老子 should be pronounced Lǎudž here instead of lǎudz, the latter meaning father in certain districts of China

15. 神-mì (-秘) SV: be mysterious—from 神 (inscrutable) and mì (secret)

16. "清淨無爲" Ph: "Quietude and noninterference"—from 清淨 (quietude) and 無爲 (noninterference), the basic philosophy of Laotse

17. 主張 V: advocate

一. 我主張這個禮拜天都到舊金山去玩兒。

18. wěi 大 (偉-) SV: be great, remarkable—a synonym compound

wěi-人 N: a great man

19. Yìn-度 (印-) PW: India (transliteration of Hindu)

20. Shṙjyāmóuní (釋迦牟尼) N: Shakyamuni (founder of Buddhism)

21. 等等 N: and so forth, and so on

22. 產業 N: property

第十四課　中國的宗教（二）

除了上一課講的三大宗教以外，中國還有兩個shr̀-力越來越大的宗教，就是回教跟Jīdū-教。在第八世紀有一次中國正有內亂的時候，一個回教國王派了四千個兵到中國來幫助中國。後來就都留在中國沒回去。現在中國信回教的人，大多數都是他們的後代。

回教又叫回回教。中國的西北部是回教shr̀-力最大的地方。

Jīdū-教在Táng Cháu就傳到中國一次。後來到明Cháu又第二次傳進來。經過幾百年的發展，後來Jīdū-教的新舊兩派一Yēsū-教跟天主教一在中國的shr̀-力都越來越大。他們除了傳教以外，還設立了很多學校，醫院，社會服務twán-體，如同青年會等等。本着Yēsū-的精神，努力twēi-動種種宗教活動跟社會服務的事情。

中國在宗教上的一個特點是：Fwó-教的myàu-裏常有道教的神像，道教的觀裏也常有Fwó-教的神像。並且有的地方發現Kǔng-子，老子跟Shr̀jyāmóuní三個神像在一塊兒。念書的人也許平常甚麽宗教都不信。可是到家裏死了人的時候，常把héshang跟道-shr 同時請來，給死人 chāudù. 現在的一種宗教理論是：各宗教拜的都是一個神。這在中國早已經實行了很久了。

因爲中國人向來對於宗教就是這種 tài-度，所以中國向來没有過甚麽宗教 jànjēng，也向來不 myǎn-chang 人信甚麽宗教。我們可以說中國是世界上一個信教最自由的國家。

（一）我們暫且別談他了，不但丢人，而且還讓人生氣。

（二）這個問題很簡單。在鄉下賣不出去，就全運進城。我敢保準賣得出去。你放心去休息吧。

（三）按我的意思，你不如借給他一點兒錢救救他。你記得他結婚的時候，你還是介紹人呢。

（四）陰天的時候，我最怕天氣熱。要是再加上亂笑亂鬧的聲音，我就簡直的不能專心念書了。

（五）你快把東西包好了，放在這兒。這兒很安全。千萬別各處亂放！三十號我一定派人來拿。

（六）中國從前一位大官說，人不但要愛惜一寸光陰，連一分光陰都要愛惜。

（七）海邊兒上有很多石頭。

（八）這個學校有些學生不喜歡的規-jyu.

(九) 我昨天收到一封信。信上說我小時候的一個女朋友已經結婚了。

(十) 你把這個拿去用吧。我另外還有一個呢。

(十一) 他說中國話說的相當好。

Vocabulary

1. 內 nèi　BF: inside, within, inner

　內人　N: my wife (polite)

　…以內　MA: within…

　一. 我內人很會作中國飯。

　二. 三年以內我不會離開這兒。

2. 亂 lwàn　SV/A: be disorderly, reckless/in disorder, recklessly

　內亂　N: civil war

　一. 這間屋子很亂。

　二. 他喜歡亂用別人的東西。

　三. 一個國家不應當有內亂。

3. 派 pài　V/N: appoint, delegate/a school of thought, a sect

　一. 政府派了三個代表去了。

　二. 你知道Yēsū-教裏有多少派嗎?

4. 助 jù　BF: help

　幫助　V/N: help

　一. 他幫助我把這些事都作完了。

　二. 念這本書對我一點兒幫助也沒有。

5. 設 shè BF: establish, arrange
6. 立 lì BF: establish; instantly
 設立 V: establish, set up
 立刻 A: at once
 一. 城裏頭設立了一個新學校。
 二. 請叫他立刻來。
7. 醫 yī BF: heal, cure
8. 院 ywàn BF: courtyard, hall, college
 醫院 N: a hospital
 院子 N: a courtyard
9. 服 fú BF: serve; clothes
 衣服 N: clothes (interchangeable with 衣-shang)
10. 務 wù BF: duty, affairs
 服務 V/N: serve/service
 一. 我哥哥在政府裏服務。
 二. 青年會是一個社會服務twán體。
11. 青 chīng SV: be green, blue, black
 男青年會 N: Y.M.C.A.
 女青年會 N: Y.W.C.A.
 青年(人) N: youth
 一. 上海有男青年會也有女青年會。
 二. 青年(人)應當爲國家服務。
12. 精 jīng BF: spirit, essence
 精神 N: spirit
 有精神 SV: be full of spirit and energy
 一. 我這幾天的精神很不好。
 二. 他說話的時候很有精神。
13. 努 nǔ BF: exert, strive
 努力 A/SV: exert one's strength/be vigorous

一. 努力學，一定學得會。

二. 我知道你們都很努力。

14. 動 dùng V: move

活動 SV/N: be active/activity

一. 請別動。

二. 他在社會上很多活動裏都很活動。

15. 相 syāng BF: mutual, reciprocal

相當 A: rather, fairly, relatively

一. 他的中國話說得相當好。

Notes

1. shr̀-力 (勢-) N: influence, power
2. 回教 N: Mohammedanism—named after one of the Turki tribes, the Ouigours (維吾爾), who brought the Mohammedan religion into China

   回回教 N: (another name for) Mohammedanism
3. Jīdū-教(基督-) N: Christianity—from <u>Jīdū</u> (Christ) and 教 (religion)
4. bīng (兵) N: soldier
5. 後代 N: descendant
6. Táng Cháu (唐朝) N: the T'ang Dynasty (618–907 A.D.)

   明 Cháu (朝) N: the Ming Dynasty (1368–1643 A.D.)
7. Yēsū-教 (耶穌-) N: Protestant Christianity—from Yēsū (Jesus) and 教 (religion)—as distinct from Roman Catholicism

天主教 N: Roman Catholicism－天主 (Lord in Heaven) is the Catholic term for God who is called 上 -dì in Protestant churches

8. twán-體 (團-) N: organization

9. 本着 CV: based on

一. 我們都應當本着愛人的精神作事。

10. twēi-動 (推-) V: promote

11. 種種 N: all sorts

一. 因爲他有種種的不方便，所以今天不來了。

12. 特點 N: special characteristics, points

一. 這種酒的特點是又好喝又便-yi。

13. myàu (廟) N: temple

14. 神像 N: an image or idol

15. 觀 N: a Taoist temple－觀 is pronounced gwàn here

16. héshang (和尚) N: a Buddhist priest－shàng is given a falling tone when stressed

17. 道-shr (-士) N: a Taoist priest－shr̀ is given a falling tone when stressed

18. chāudù (超渡) V: release souls from suffering, raise from a state of suffering in the next world

19. tài-度 (態-) N: attitude

20. jànjēng (戰爭) N: war

21. myǎnchyǎng (勉強) V: compel

22. 而且 A: moreover, besides (interchangeable with 並且)

一. 我們在中國城玩兒了一天，而且還

吃了一次中國飯。

23. 敢保 V: guarantee

一. 你要是天天念書，我敢保你念得很好。

24. 不如 CV/V: not as good as/had better (interchangeable with 最好 in the second sense)

一. 我的中國話不如他的好。

二. 我們不如走吧。天黑了，別等了。

25. 介紹人 N: introducer

26. 專心 A/SV: with undivided attention

一. 我們都應當專心學中文。

二. 他念書很專心。

27. 安全 SV/N: be safe, secure/safety, security

一. 住在這兒最安全。

二. 爲了你家的安全，你不如bān-到城裏頭來住。

Tien T'ang, Temple of Heaven PEKING

第十五課　長城跟運河

中國最有名的兩個工-chéng是長城跟運河。連在全世界都是非常有名的。兩千多年以前，有幾個靠北部的國家各在北部建-jù城牆，保護自己的國家，fáng-備北方的yóumù-民-dzú.等到紀-ywán-前第三世紀中國tǔng-一以後，才把這些城牆連接起來，成了一條長城。後來又修-jù-了很多次。一直到四五百年以前還大規模的修-jù-過一次呢。

長城從河北省到Gānsu-省一共長五千多里。因爲這麽長，所以另外一個名稱是萬里長城。長城高三十尺，寬十尺到二十尺。用造長城的tsáilyàu可以建-jù一個高八尺，寬三尺，wéi-着地-chyóu ràu一-jōu的城牆。長城没有問題的可以說是全世界最長最大的牆。

中國第二個大工-chéng是運河。運河北頭兒到河北省的通縣，南頭兒到Jè-江省的Háng-縣。一共長一千四百四十公里。這條運河不都是用人工作成的。有幾部分是原來的河。從紀-ywán-前第五世紀起，就起-shř-了這個大工-chéng.紀-ywán-後第七世紀，第一次大規模的把幾條原來的河連接起來。一直到第十三世紀快完的時候，才完成了這條長一千四百多公里的運河。一共用了一千七百多年。

世界上還有兩條出名的運河。一條是Sūyíshr̀運河，只長一百六十六公里。另外一條是Bā-拿馬運河，只長八十一公里。並且兩條運河剛完成了不到一百年。所以，中國的運河實在是世界上最老最長的運河。

從前在中國還没修鐵路的時候，南北的交通跟運-shū多半都靠着這條運河。中國北部出產的米很少，所以特別是北方的米要靠着運河從南方運來。

中國wā運河是爲了交通運-shū的原故；造長城是爲了政治jyūn-事的原故。不管是爲了甚麽原故，運河跟長城都稱得起是中國的兩個最大的工-chéng.

（一）花燈雖然没有電燈亮，可是好看。所以我給我姐姐買了一個紅的，給我妹妹買了一個黄的。

（二）那件事我知道的很清楚。有機會我把結果詳詳細細的告訴你。

（三）樹後面就是我家。請進來坐坐。

（四）這間屋子氣味很大。你爲甚麽選了這麽一個地方放行李？我勸你快拿走。

（五）你給我任何代價我也不作這麽危險的事。

(六) 人說西洋金子沒有中國金子好。這恐怕沒有甚麼根據吧。金子永遠是好的。

(七) 大使館五號那天爲新大使開了一個歡迎會。人多極了，連車都沒地方停。

(八) 現在皮子賤了。這塊厚的才十塊錢，也很亮，並且不喜歡還可以送回去。

(九) 這個圓的比那個方的大一倍。一定很佔地方。

(十) 他跟普通人不一樣。有很多非常怪的地方。比方說，跟他借書，他也一定要收據。

(十一) 他的性情很好，努力作事，也很合作。

(十二) 這個土山上的風景很有名。

(十三) 他那個人要錢不要命。

(十四) 各國有各國的俗話。

Vobabulary

1. 靠 kàu V: depend on; be near to; [lean on]

 可靠 SV: be reliable

 一. 這件事你得自己作，別靠別人。

 二. 他很可靠你可以請他幫忙。

 三. 中國靠西北部有很多高山。

2. 建 jyàn BF: establish, erect

3. 牆 chyáng N: wall

 城牆 N: the wall of a city

4. 護 hù BF: protect

保護 V: protect

一. 男人應當保護女人。

5. 修 syōu V: repair

一. 我就會開車，不會修車。

6. 模 mwó BF: pattern, style

規模 N: scale, scope

一. 我們這個學校規模很大。

7. 省 shěng N/V: province/save (economize)

省錢 SV/VO: be economical /save money

省事 SV/VO: trouble-saving/save trouble

省得 CV: lest, in order to prevent (someone from doing something)

河北省 PW: Hopei Province

一. 我這個辦法又省錢又省事。

二. 最好你去，省得他來。

三. 我替你買，可以給你省很多錢。

8. 里 lǐ M: (a Chinese measurement of distance about one-third of a mile)

9. 尺 chř N/M: a foot rule/(a Chinese foot divided into ten inches roughly equivalent to forteen English inches)

一. 中國尺每尺有十寸。

10. 寬 kwān SV: be broad, wide

一. 這條河很長，可是不很寬。

11. 縣 syàn N: a hsien, district (roughly equivalent to a county in the U.S.)

一 這個縣有四個中學。

12. 公 gūng BF: public; official (adj.)

公里 M: a kilometer

公事 N: official business

公事房(兒) N: office

一. 我現在得到公事房(兒)去，有很多公事要辦。

13. 鐵 tyě N: iron

鐵路 N: a railway

一. 火車必得在鐵路上走。

14. 交 jyāu BF/V: give; communicate/befriend

交給 V: hand over to, give to

交通 N: communications

交朋友 VO: make friends with

一. 你把錢交給誰了？

二. 美國的鐵路交通發展得很快。

三. 我最喜歡交朋友。

15. 治 jr̀ BF: govern

政治 N: politics

一. 法國的政治很亂。

Notes

1. 長城 PW: the Great Wall (of China) propularly known as the 萬里長城
2. 運河 PW: the Grand Canal (of China); a canal
3. 工-chéng (-程) N: construction work, engineering
4. 建-jù (-築) V/N: construct/construction
5. fáng-備 (防-) V: guard against
6. yóumù-民-dzú (遊牧民族) N: nomad tribe

7. tǔng-一 (統-) V/N: unify/unity
8. 連接 V: join
   一. 那條運河把大西洋跟太平洋連接起來了。
9. 修-jù (-築) V: repair, build
10. Gānsù-省(甘肅-) PW: the province of Kansu in Northwestern China (肅 is pronounced sù
11. tsáilyàu (材料) N: material
12. wéi-着 (圍-) V: surround
13. 地-chyóu (-球) N: the earth, the globe
14. ràu-一-jōu (繞一週) Ph: wind around once
15. 北頭兒 N: the northern terminal
    南頭兒 N: the southern terminal
16. 通縣 PW: T'unghsien—a town at the northern end of the Grand Canal in Hopei Province
17. Jè-江省 (浙-) PW: the province of Chekiang in East China
18. Háng-縣 (杭-) PW: Hang-hsien, the provincial capital of Chekiang
19. Sūyíshr̀ 運河 (蘇彝士) PW: the Suez Canal
20. Bā-拿馬運河(巴-) PW: the Panama Canal
21. 完成 V: accomplish, complete
    一. 那個工作已經完成很久了。
22. 運-shū (-輸) V/N: transport/transportation
23. wā (挖-) V: dig
24. jyūn-事 (軍-) N: military matters, military

25. 稱得起 RV: worthy of being called (this resultative verb is only used in its affirmative potential form)

一. 他真稱得起是一位好人。

26. 氣味 N: odor

27. 大使館 N: embassy

大使 N: ambassador

28. 歡迎會 N: a welcome meeting

29. 收據 N: a receipt

Great Wall of China
Wàn-lǐ Cháng-chéng

第十六課　甚麽是國語

有很多外國人怕學中國話，因爲中國各處說的話不同。在一個地方費了很多事學了一種話，還是不會說—也聽不懂—其餘的地方的話。這一點兒也不奇怪。Ōujou也是這個樣子。兩國離着才有幾百yīng-里，可是說的話就不一樣了。

中國話最重要的是：Wú-語，Mǐn-語，Ywè-語跟國語。江-sū Jè-江兩省是Wú-語的勢力範圍。Fú-建Táiwān兩省是Mǐn-語的勢力範圍。Gwǎng-東Gwǎng-西兩省是Ywè-語的勢力範圍。其餘各省從東北的Jílín一直到西南的Yún-南都是國語的勢力範圍。不算Ménggǔ跟西-dzàng中國各省這八百七十多萬方公里的地方，十分-jr-九以上都是說國語的地帶。八萬萬人裏每十個人有七個人都住在這一個地帶。我們可以知道國語的範圍多麽大了。

在這麽大的國語地帶裏，各地方的人說話雖然彼此聽得懂，可是口音不一樣。就如同美國南部有南部的口音，Nyǒuywē-市裏Bùkèlín有Bùkèlín-的口音一樣。另外再加上幾種彼此聽不懂的話，真是一個統一的國家的大jàngài. 於是從第十七世紀起就推行國語。希望全國都說一種話。到了民國以後，政府更注重這個運動。現在全國各處的學校都教國語。全國說國語的人越來越多。

甚麼是國語？簡單的回答：國語的百分-jr-九十以上都是北-jīng話.因爲北-jīng是最近這幾百年中國的國都,所以北-jīng.話是全國最普通的話。有時候有中國別的地方的人反對這個辦法。他們說爲甚麼只有北-jīng話才算國語呢？難道我們說的話不是中國話嗎？其實，中國各省的話都是中國話。要打算統一國語，各處都說一種話，就非要選出一個最普通的話來推行不可。國語的「國」跟國貨的「國」不是一個意思。國貨的「國」是中國的意思；不是國貨就不是中國貨。國語的「國」要是這個意思，不會說國語的中國人當然可以不高-syìng.可是國語的「國」跟國歌的「國」是一個意思，是全國的意思。國歌是全國要唱的一個歌；國語是全國要說的一種話。

（一）無論甚麼都可以。隨便預備一點兒就成了。涼的我也吃。

（二）設立一個醫院不是小事。一切都要先商量商量。

（三）有些地方自殺變成了一種很常見的事。活着一沒意思，就總是要跳河，跳湖，跳海或是跳火山。

（四）人不應當分黨分派。都應當本着彼此幫助的精神，為社會服務，使社會越來越進步。

（五）只有那塊石頭旁邊兒還乾淨，可以在那兒休息一會兒。可是有一點兒太陽。

（六）青年會在春天跟秋天的時候，有各類的活動，如同電影兒跟各種研究會甚麽的。

（七）我的記性真壞！念了一整夜的書，第二天一句也不會背了，並且連「木」這個字都不認識了。

（八）我祖父替我起的那個名子，後來我父親又給我改了。我現在用的這個名子是我自己起的。

（九）大概鄉下的人口少一點兒。

（十）我向來沒有不好的習-gwàn。

（十一）他除了有產業以外，還有很多朋友。

Vocabulary

1. 語 yǔ　BF: language
　國語　N: the Chinese national language
2. 費 fèi　V: waste
　費錢　SV/VO: be expensive, wasteful/cost money
　費事　SV/VO: be troublesome/take a lot of work
　費時候　SV/VO: be time consuming/take time
　一. 有人因爲結婚要費很多錢，所以就不結婚。
　二. 學中文很費事，對不對？
　三. 交女朋友真費時候。
3. 其 chí　BF: his, her, its, their
　其實　MA: actually, as a matter of fact
　一. 人都說他有錢，其實他並沒甚麽錢。
4. 餘 yú　BF: remainder
　其餘　N: the rest, the surplus
　一. 我就喜歡這一本書。其餘的我都不要。
5. 勢 shr̀　BF: power, influence
　勢力　N: strength, influence
　一. 天主教在外國的勢力很大。
6. 範 fàn　BF: a pattern, rule
7. 圍 wéi　BF: surround, circumference
　範圍　N: sphere, jurisdiction
　一. 青年會的工作範圍很大。
8. 彼 bǐ　BF: he, she, the other
9. 此 tsž　BF this, here
　彼此　N: mutual, you and I, both parties
　一. 要是我們能合作，彼此都有好處。

10. 市 shr̀ BF: municipality

一. 北京市有很多有名的學校。

11. 統 tǔng BF: control

統一 V/N: unify/unity

一. 統一國語不是一件容易事。

12. 推 twēi V: push

推行 V: carry into operation

一. 我們應當努力推行這個運動。

13. 答 dá BF: answer

回答 V: answer

一. 我問了他很多話,他一句也沒回答。

14. 反 fǎn BF: oppose, be contrary to

反正 MA: in any case, anyway (wrong or right)

反對 V: oppose

一. 別再說了。反正我不信你的話。

二. 他們都反對你的意思。

15. 貨 hwò N: goods

國貨 N: native products

洋貨 N: imported goods

一. 中國自己出的貨我們叫國貨;外國運來的我們叫洋貨。

Notes

1.	yīng-里 (英-)	M:	a mile
2.	Wú-語 (吳-)	N:	the Wu dialect which includes the various dialects of the Kiangsu and Chekiang provinces
3.	Mǐn-語 (閩-)	N:	the Fukien dialect which includes the various dialects of the province of Fukien
4.	Ywè-語 (粵-)	N:	the Cantonese dialect which includes the various dialects of Kwangtung and Kwangsi provinces
5.	江-sū, Jè-江 (-蘇) (浙-)	PW:	the provinces of Kiangsu and Cheki-ang in East China
6.	Fú-建, Táiwān (福-) (台灣)	PW:	the provinces of Fukien and Taiwan (Formosa) in Southeastern China
7.	Gwǎng-東, Gwǎng-西 (廣-) (廣-)	PW:	the provinces of Kwangtung and Kwangsi in South China
8.	Jílín (吉林)	PW:	the province of Kirin in Northeastern China
9.	Yún-南 (雲-)	PW:	the province of Yunnan in Southwest-ern China
10.	Ménggǔ (蒙古)	PW:	Mongolia
11.	西-dzàng (-藏)	PW:	Tibet
12.	方公里	M:	a square kilometer
13.	地帶	N:	area, region
14.	口音	N:	accent (in pronunciation) 一. 他說話有南方口音。
15.	Nyǒuywē-市 (紐約-)	PW:	the City of New York

16. Bùkèlín (布克林) PW: Brooklyn
17. jàngài (障礙) N: obstacle
18. 於是 MA: then, thereupon
    一. 誰都不喜歡聽他說笑話，於是他就不說了。
19. 運動 N: movement
    一. 社會上的好運動，我們都應當幫助推行。
20. 難道 MA: Do you mean to say?, Is it conceivable?
    一. 難道你連一塊錢也没有嗎？
21. 分黨分派 Ph: to form cliques—lit. divide into parties and schools
    一. 我們要是希望合作就不能分黨分派。
22. 研究會 N: a study group
    一. 青年會常有各種研究會的活動。

Great Hall of the People PEKING

第十七課　國語四聲

中文一共有差不多四萬個字，可是國語只有差不多四百個字音。平·jyūn 每一個字音有一百個字。每一個字音又分成四聲，於是同音同聲的字就減少到二十五個那麽多。四聲是中文發音必得有的一部分。說話的時候一定要說的很準；要不然「看書」可能說成「kǎn 樹」，客氣話會變成很不客氣的話。比方說「您太客氣」這句話，一說不準就可能變成「您太可氣」。

同音同聲的字雖然減少到平·jyūn 二十五個，可是還是太多。人說「勢力」這兩個字的時候，你不知道他說的是「勢力」，是「市立」。這麽說，中國話好像很難 shr· 的。其實，說話的時候因爲有上下文的關·syi，很少有這種情形。「他很有勢力」這句話裏，一定是「勢力」這兩個字，不是「市立」這兩個字。「市立中學」的「市立」兩個字，一定不是「勢力」這兩個字。

國語現在用的四聲是：陰平，陽平，上聲跟去聲。陰平是一個高而平的聲音；陽平是一個從相當高的音起，再升高的聲音；上聲從低升高；去聲從高降低。陰平的聲音是一個音高；其餘的三個聲音都不是一個音高。所以說話的時候，聲音按照四聲的特性，忽高忽低，上來下去，造出一個說話的sywánlyù來。不懂中國話的人聽中國人說話像唱歌shr-的，就是因爲這個原故。

因爲中國話裏有這個說話的sywánlyù,所以中國作-chyǔ-家作-chyǔ的時候,寫出來的音樂sywánlyù-線,必得跟這個說話sywánlyù-線相合。高的地方要跟着高，低的地方要跟着低，要不然四聲唱出來就都亂了。「郵政局」可能唱成「有證據」。這並不是隨便亂講空話的。在「九一八」那個kàngjàn歌-chyǔ-裏,因爲「九一八」那三個字的音樂sywánlyù作的跟說話的sywánlyù不相合,所以唱起來聽着像"jyōu yǐba."

現在我們知道了四聲在中國話裏的重要了。不管是說話還是唱歌兒，四聲都要非常準。四聲是中國話的一個特色；四聲使中國話變成世界上一種音樂的話。

(一) 讓我休息一會兒吧。我最怕熱鬧。
(二) 請你把你大衣的尺寸放在信封兒裏給我留下。
(三) 有的宗教向來不傳教；有的宗教主張傳教。我說兩種看法都有理由。

(四) 別人有危險的時候，我們不能只是在旁邊兒看着不救。

(五) 你暫時先別走，不久他就回來。回來以後，我一定給你介紹。你可以跟他談談你所研究的商業問題。

(六) 他剛結婚就買了一個新式的房子。那個地方是新發展的。風景很好，也很安全。

(七) 今天晚上要降到二十多度。我內人說我shēn-體不好。讓我出去的時候穿厚一點兒的衣服。

(八) 東西太多，我不敢說包得上包不上。要是在路上開了，那才丢人呢。

(九) 華光樓是一個專爲有錢的人吃飯的地方。可惜我沒錢，沒機會去吃飯。

(十) 你說那個官死了。你有甚麽根據嗎？

(十一) 我tsān-觀了一個城。城裏的路很寬。

(十二) 各國不但說話不同，風俗也不同。

Vocabulary

1. 減 jyǎn V: decrease; subtract

   減少 V: reduce, diminish

   一. 三減二是一。

   二. 你這麽作可以減少很多máfan.

2. 您 nín N: you (polite form)

   一. 小孩子跟大人說話的時候應當說「您」。

3. 形 syíng BF: figure, form

   情形 N: condition, situation

   一. 您可以告訴我一點兒中國的情形嗎?

4. 升 shēng BF: ascend, rise

   升高 RV: ascend, rise

   一. 天氣熱的時候, wēn-度就升高。

5. 低 dī SV/V: be low/lower

   低頭 VO: bow the head

   一. 這張桌子爲我用太低。

   二. Chídǎu 的時候要低頭。

6. 降 jyàng BF: descend

   降低 RV: drop lower

   一. 明天的wēn-度要降低十度。

7. 照 jàu V/CV: reflect/according to

   照像 VO: take photographs

   照像機 N: camera

   按照 CV: according to (interchangeable with 按着 or 照着)

   一. 我的照像機壞了。這兩天我没出去照像。

二. 按照你的意思，是不是我們一塊兒去？

8. 忽 hū　BF: suddenly
忽然　MA: suddenly
忽高忽低　Ph: now high, now low
一. 他正在說着話忽然就哭了。
二. 他唱歌兒的聲音忽高忽低，真不好聽。

9. 樂 ywè/[lè]　BF: music/[happiness]
音樂　N: music
一. 研究音樂的人都喜歡音樂。

10. 線 syàn　N: thread; line; wire
無線電　N: radio

11. 郵 yóu　BF: postal
郵費　N: postage
郵差　N: mail man (note 差 is pronounced <u>chāi</u> here)

12. 局 jyú　BF: an office, a bureau
郵(政)局　N: post-office
電報局　N: telegraph office
電話局　N: telephone office

13. 證 jèng　BF: evidence, proof
證據　N: documentary proof, a proof

14. 空 kūng　SV: be empty
空話　N: empty talk
空氣　N: air
空屋子　N: vacant room
一. 那間是空屋子，沒人住。

15. 色 sè　BF: color; quality
特色　N: unique feature
一. 他寫的這本書有甚麼特色？

Notes

1. 字音 N: pronunciation of a written character
   一. 我認識這個字，可是字音念不準。
2. 平-jyūn (-均) A: on the average
3. 同音同聲 Ph: having the same sound and tone
4. 發音 VO/N: pronounce/pronunciation
   一. 在發音以前，先要看看是哪一聲。
   二. 這個學生的發音不準。
5. kǎn-樹 (砍-) VO: cut down a tree
6. 可氣 SV: be provoking
   一. 這個孩子真可氣，天天不念書。
7. 市立 (學校) N: municipal (school)
8. 上下文 N: the context
   一. 不認識這個字不要緊，一看上下文就懂了。
9. 四聲 N: the four tones of the Chinese-Mandarin spoken language
   陰平 N: the first or (high) level tone
   一. 「張」是一個陰平字。
   陽平 N: the second or (high) rising tone
   一. 「王」是一個陽平字。
   上聲 N: the third or low (rising) tone—上 is pronounced shǎng here because it designates the low tone
   一. 上聲的「上」字應當念第三聲。
   去聲 N: the fourth or (high) falling tone
   一. 去聲的「去」字是一個去聲字。
10. 音高 N: pitch (music)
11. 特性 N: characteristics

一. 這個東西的特性是不怕水。

12. sywánlyù (旋律) N: melody

sywánlyù-線 N: melodic line

13. 作-chyǔ-家 (-曲-) N: composer

作-chyǔ (-曲) VO: compose—lit. make a musical composition

14. 相合 SV: agree, coincide

一. 你說的這個故事前後不相合。

15. "九一八" N: September 18th (1931 when Japan invaded Manchuria)—name of a well-known patriotic song

16. kàngjàn 歌-chyǔ (抗戰歌曲) N: songs sung during and about the War of Resistance (referring to the Sino-Japanese War, 1937-1945)

17. jyōu yǐba (揪尾巴) VO: grab by the tail

18. 語-yán (-言) N: language

19. 尺寸 N: length—lit. feet and inches (尺 is pronounced chŕ here instead of chř)

一. 請您把那張畫兒的尺寸寫下來

20. 理由 N: reason

一. 他今天忽然走了, 一定有理由。

21. 旁邊兒 PW: by the side of

一. 你旁邊兒坐着的那個人是誰?

第十八課　中國文字

中國這幾千年有一個很困難的問題，一直到現在没能圓滿的解決。這個問題就是文-máng問題。爲甚麽中國大多數的人都不識字呢？主要的原故是因爲中國文字太難。

中國字的形-jwàng是方的；没有字母，不能pīn-音。字的組織很複雜，跟世界上任何種文字都不一樣。有的字原來是代表東西的形-jwàng:「日」「月」這些字屬於這一類。有的字你一看就知道是甚麽意思:「上」「下」這些字屬於這一類。有的字部-shǒu部分告訴我們字的大意，其餘部分規定字的聲音:「洋」「湖」這些字屬於這一類。這只是三類。中國字一共分六大類，叫「六書」。

中國字寫起來的時候，要一筆一畫的寫。「一」字筆畫很簡單，只有一畫。可是最複雜的字有三十五畫那麽多。常用的字平-jyūn每一個字有十畫。

因爲中國字不用字母，所以在字典裏決定哪個字在前頭，哪個字在後頭的時候，必得用别的方法。解決這個問題的一個最普通的方法是：把所有的中國字分成二百一十四部。拿每一部各字相同的部分作那部的部-shǒu. 查字典的時候，先要知道一個字在甚麽部，然後再在字典上那一部裏，按照筆畫的多少找那個字。所以中國字不但難認，難寫，並且還難查。

解決文-máng問題有兩種方法。第一種方法是改革中國文字，就是：或是限-jr̀常用字，或是提-chàng簡體字，或是用國語-lwó-馬字。國語-lwó-馬字這個方法，問題複雜，困難太多。因爲文字跟國家的文化有很大的關-syi，所以很多人反對完全改用國語-lwó-馬字。第二種解決的方法是推行識字運動。從前中國已經努力推行過很多次。現在還是努力的推行。

不論實行甚麽方法，人人都應當識字這件事在每一個國家裏非常重要。一個國家的文-máng要是太多，實在影-syǎng國家的進步。

（一）一個國家交通的好壞，要靠公路鐵路修的多不多。要是多，就不知道要方便多少倍。

（二）人民永遠歡迎保護人民的政府。要是政府的官只愛錢，不作事，國家的政治就壞了。

（三）這種水果價錢不高。皮兒是黃的，很好看，可是味兒不大好。我勸你別因爲賤就買。

（四）那縣真稱得起是一個模範縣。雖然城牆是土的，可是城裏有電燈，電話跟自來水。街上很乾淨，還有很多花兒。

（五）我妹妹恐怕知道的不清楚。我姐姐可以詳細的告訴您。

（六）老李去年跟我借的金表還没給我呢。你看多不體面！他這麽作事，非改不可。

（七）月亮已經上了東山，好像停在那兒不動的樣子。

（八）我們那帶地方，米佔一切出產的三分·jr·一。

（九）紀小姐三號來。我們不如都去接他。

（十）那塊紅石頭沒丟。我收起來了。

（土）我祖父活了一百歲才死。

（当）這兩個椅子的中間太寬了吧。

II. Evolution of mǎ 'horse' and yú 'fish'

mǎ 

Shang Dynasty (about 1500–1028 B.C.). Earliest known form, found on bronze vessels and oracle bones.

About 200 B.C. "Small Seal" characters developed in the Ch'in Dynasty (221–206 B.C.)

About 100 A.D. "Model Script," a standardized form which replaced the previous variety of styles and has continued in use to the present.

Vocabulary

1. 困 kwùn BF: difficulty, hardship

   困難 SV/N: be difficult/difficulty, hardship

   一. 我們剛學中文的時候，覺得發音很困難。

   二. 現在你們還有困難嗎？

2. 滿 mǎn SV: be full

   圓滿 SV: be satisfactory

   一. 車裏的水滿了，別再加了。

   二. 昨天我們談話的結果很圓滿。

3. 解 jyě V: loosen, untie

4. 决 jywé BF: decide, decidedly

   解决 V: solve

   决定 V: decide

   一. 我想這個問題沒法子解决。

   二. 他决定明年回國。

5. 組 dzǔ BF: organize

6. 織 jr̄ V: weave; knit

   組織 V/N: organize/organization

   一. 我母親給我織了一件毛衣(sweater).

   二. 組織政府的時候，要越簡單越好。

   三. 青年會是一個很好的組織。

7. 複 fù BF: complex

8. 雜 dzá SV: be mixed; miscellaneous

   複雜 SV: be complex (as contrasted with 簡單)

   一. 這個問題很複雜。

9. 屬 shǔ V: belong to, be subject to

   屬於 V: belong to

一. 這些書都屬於一類。

10. 典 dyǎn BF: law, code

字典 N: dictionary

一. 你會用中文字典嗎?

11. 查 chá V: investigate, search into

查字典 VO: consult the dictionary

一. 請查一查明天是十幾號?

二. 查中文字典是很複雜的一件事。

12. 革 gé BF: remove, change

改革 V/N: reform

一. 改革舊風俗不是一件容易事。

二. 進步的社會常常有改革。

13. 限 syàn BF: limit, boundary

14. 提 tí BF: raise, lift in the hand

15. 化 hwà BF: transform

文化 N: culture, civilization

一. 在這個學校念一年中文, 可以懂得很多中國文化。

III. Examples of Chinese Characters

(The first form shown is the modern form; the second is the earliest known form.)

1. 馬
2. 魚
3. 人
4. 大
5. 天
6. 水
7. 山
8. 日
9. 月
10. 中

Notes

1. 文字 N: characters, writing
   一. 中國文字比西洋各國文字都難。
2. 文-máng (-盲) N: illiteracy; an illiterate—lit. literary blind
3. 識字 VO: recognize characters—a more concise form derived from 認識字
4. 主要 SV: be essential
   一. 我們最好先討論最主要的問題。
5. 形-jwàng (-狀) N: form, appearance
6. 字母 N: letters (of an alphabet)
   一. 可惜中國文字沒有字母，所以很難。
7. pīn-音 (拼-) VO: spell phonetically
8. 部-shǒu (-首) N: radicals (for Chinese characters)
9. 大意 N: the general idea
   一. 看那本書的時候，只明白大意就行了。
10. 規定 V/N: regulate/regulation
    一. 已經規定好了，我們明天一塊兒走。
    二. 那些規定都是他的意思。
11. 六書 N: the six categories into which Chinese characters are divided:
    (1) Syàngsyíng (象形), containing representations of objects like 日 and 月
    (2) Jřshr̀ (指事), containing those whose form indicates the meaning, as 上 and 下
    (3) Hwèiyì (會意), characters the

construction of which suggests the meaning, as 明 and 信

(4) Syéshēng or syíngshēng (諧聲 or 形聲), the radical gives the idea of the meaning and the other part the sound, as 洋 and 湖

(5) Jyǎjyè (假借), containing characters used only for their sounds, as 令 and 汝

(6) Jwǎnjù (轉注), characters which have more than one sound, the meaning of which also changes with the sound, as 考 and 老

12. 筆畫 N: strokes (in writing characters)

一筆一畫的 Ph: stroke by stroke

一. 筆畫多的字很難寫。

二. 你寫的字太不清楚。請一筆一畫的寫。

13. 限-jr̀(-制) V: limit, restrict

14. 簡體字 N: simplified characters

15. 國語-lwó-馬字 (-羅-) N: Chinese-Mandarin romanization

16. 公路 N: public highway

一. 美國每年修很多公路。

17. 模範縣 N: a model hsien

模範 N: model (in the sense of being exemplary)

一. 定縣雖然小，可是是一個模範縣。

二. 他母親是所有的母親的模範。

第十九課　中國飯

中國人吃飯跟美國人吃飯，在思想上好像有一個很大的不同的地方。中國人專講究味兒，只注意好吃不好吃。可是美國人多半講究吃的東西對於身體有甚麽好處。也不是不注意味兒，可是没有中國人那麽注意。

中國人吃飯除了注意吃的味兒以外，還注意聞的味兒，也講究好看不好看。所以我們决定一個菜好不好，要看那個菜的「色」「syāng」「味」怎麽樣。「色」就是yán色；「syāng」就是syāng-味兒，也就是聞的味兒；「味」就是吃的味兒。

甚麽是好吃，甚麽是不好吃呢？這個問題很難回答。有人說，很多東西人不愛吃，是因爲没有吃的習-gwàn.吃的時候覺得味兒特別，就不喜歡。要是肯lyàn-習，常常吃，慢慢的就會覺得好吃了。也有人說，好吃的東西就是好吃，不好吃的東西就是不好吃。比方說，特別kǔ-的東西誰愛吃！我想這兩種說法也許都對。

我們既然没法子規定甚麽好吃，甚麽不好吃，所以是中國飯好吃，還是美國飯好吃，我們也没法子知道。但是我們準知道美國飯簡單，中國飯複雜。中國飯怎麼複雜呢？第一,菜的種類複雜；第二，作菜的方法複雜。先說菜的種類。中國人請客的時候，一桌菜常有四五十樣兒。就是平常家裏吃飯,差不多也都是四個菜一個 tāng. 再說，冬天有冬天的菜，夏天有夏天的菜。天氣冷，吃熱的；天氣熱，吃温 -he- 的,或是吃涼的。菜的樣子多，可以常常 hwàn- 着吃。

作菜的方法呢？一件最要緊的事就是「切」。中國飯在作以前，一定要切好。應該切成片兒的不能切成塊兒。片兒應當多厚，塊兒應當多大，都跟怎麼作有關 -syi. 因爲中國人以爲，要是作肉,得讓味兒進到肉裏去。這樣，中國人才覺得好吃。你要是不信，下星期我們放假的時候，請你星期六中午到我家來。讓我太太給你作一次午飯，你就知道我說的不是假的了。

（一）海口的商業向來比內地的商業發 -dá.

（二）無論建設甚麼事業，一定得有不怕難的精神，並且心裏要總有希望。

（三）江西省跟河北省中間，大概有三千多公里。到底準有多少里，我記不清楚了。我預備查一查。

(四) 青年人多半都有服務社會，服務國家的精神。

(五) 我的心常跳。有時候跳一整夜。**越**想睡**越**睡不着。春天跟秋天更壞。我得到醫院去查查。

(六) 他派我去替他買貨。我到鄉下去費了很多工夫，没選着甚麽好的。

(七) 統一國語這個問題，我研究了很久。覺得背景太複雜，範圍也太大。一個人的力量實在不夠。

(八) 連他也說這張畫兒不好。你現在又另外加上了幾句。我只好决定不買了。

(九) 人要是都能彼此幫助，社會就平安了。

(十) 那個市立中學課-shr̀-裏的光線不好。

(土) 鄉下人用陰-lì的多，用陽-lì的少。

(土) 有的新式卓子不是用木頭作的。

(圭) 可惜有些作tsźchì的法子没傳留下來。

Vocabulary

1. 身 shēn BF/M: the body/(for suits of clothes)
   - 身體 N: the body; health
   - 動身 VO: start on a journey
   - 一. 他的身體很好。
   - 二. 我們今天晚上動身。
2. 聞 wén V/BF: smell/hear
   - 聞得見 RV: can smell (it)
   - 新聞 N: news
   - 一. 讓我聞聞是甚麽味兒。
   - 二. 我聞不見有甚麽不好的味兒。
   - 三. 今天有甚麽新聞嗎?
3. 肯 kěn AV: willing, consent to
   - 一. 他不是不能作, 是不肯作。
4. 既 jì BF: since, inasmuch as
   - 既然 MA: since (it is so)
   - 一. 既然你去, 我就不必去了。
5. 冬 dūng BF: winter
   - 冬天 TW: the winter
   - 一. 冬天我不喜歡出門。
6. 夏 syà BF: summer
   - 夏天 TW: the summer
   - 一. 這兒夏天不太熱。
7. 冷 lěng SV: be cold
   - 一. 天冷了, 要多穿一點兒衣服。
8. 温 wēn BF: warm; review (lessons)
   - 温度 N: degree of temperature
   - 温習 V: review
   - 一. 屋子裏的温度不應當太高。

二. 他天天晚上温習白天念的書。

9. 該 gāi AV: ought to, should

(應)該 AV: ought to, should (interchangeable with 應當)

該你了 IE: It's your turn

一. 我已經去過了一次了。現在該你了。

10. 片 pyàn BF: slice

切成片兒 Ph: cut to slices (切 is pronounced chyē here)

(syàngpyār)像片兒 N: a photograph, snapshot

11. 肉 ròu N: meat, flesh

12. 星 syīng BF: a star, planet

13. 期 chī BF: period, date

星期 N: week (interchangeable with 禮拜)

星期日 or 星期天 TW: Sunday

一. 星期日, 星期天, 禮拜日, 禮拜天都是一天。

14. 假 jyà BF: leave of absence, vacation

放假 VO: give a vacation, holiday

請假 VO: ask for leave of absence

一. 你明天不必請假, 因爲明天放假。

15. 午 wǔ BF: noon

上午,中午,下午 TW: forenoon, noon and afternoon

午飯 N: the noon meal (interchangeable with 中飯)

一. 今天上午不上課, 下午才上課呢。

二. 我天天中午不吃午飯。

Notes

1. 思想 N: thought
   一. 他的思想很chí-怪。
2. 不同 SV: be different (more literary than 不一樣)
   一. 我看不出來這兩個人有甚麽不同的地方。
3. 注意 V/VO: pay attention
   一. 我說話的時候，請你注一點兒意。
   二. 他們都很注意這件事情。
4. 好處 N: good point, benefit
   一. 請你告訴我喝酒有甚麽好處。
5. “色”,“syāng,”“味” (香) N: color, aroma and taste
6. syāng-味兒(香-) N: aroma, fragrance
   一. 這個syāng-水兒的syāng-味兒很特別。
7. lyàn-習 (練-) V: exercise, practise
8. 說法 N: way of speaking
   一. 我們的說法不同，可是意思一樣。
9. 種類 N: kind, species
   一. 他作的菜種類很多。
10. 方法 N: way, method (interchangeable with 法子)
    一. 有很多方法請他替你作這件事。
11. 一卓菜 Nu-M-N: all the courses to be served on one table—lit. one tableful of food
12. 温-hé (-和) SV: be lukewarm— 和 is pronounced hé when stressed.

13. 切 V: cut; slice—it is pronounced chyē here

一. 切肉有很多不同的方法。

14. 塊兒 N: lump, piece, clod

一. 請你再給我一小塊兒肉。

15. 以爲 V: think, regard

一. 他以爲他很好看，其實他並不好看。

16. 內地 N: the interior (of a country)

一. 中國內地的交通很困難。

17. 發-dá (-達) SV: be developed, prosperous

18. 建設 V/N: establish, institute/what has been established or instituted

一. 政府跟人民合作,建設了很多學校。

二. 美國在各方面的建設很多。

19. 事業 N: career, profession

一. 各人的事業不同。

20. 光線 N: ray of light, light

一. 屋子裏的光線不夠。應該把電燈開開。

第二十課　民主跟中國

平常一談到民主這兩個字，我們就想到選擧這件事。民主要是只是由人民選擧政府的意思，那麽民主在中國還是一個很新的思想。可是這兩個字要是人民是最主要的意思，那麽中國在世界上已經是好幾千年的民主國家了。

Lín- 肯總統給民主政府的定義是:「民有，民治，民 -syǎng.」意思是：政府是人民的，被人民管理的，爲人民求 fú- 利的。中國這幾千年的政府，雖然不是「民有」，「民治」，可是没有問題的是「民-syǎng」的政府，人民同意存在，才能存在的政府。

現在談一談中國這幾千年的民主。第一，從兩千年以前，中國取消了封建制度，一直到現在，中國的社會都是一個没有 jyējí 的社會。第二，中國這一千五百年所實行的考試制度，使每人，無論有錢沒錢，都有機會參加考試。考取了以後都可以作官。所以有一句俗話說:「將相本無種」。第三，很古的時候中國的一個政治理論就是: hwángdì 是「受命於天」來治理人民的。要是不好好的治理，就自動的丢了天給他的治理 -chywán 人民就可以革命。第四，hwángdì 雖然在理論上專制，可是有 yùshř

來jyānchá 政府。Yùshř jyānchá-的是hwángdì跟官，而不是人民。第五，中國向來注重人民的意思。在紀-ywán-前二十三世紀的時候就有這麽一句話：「天由人民的yǎnjing看，由人民的ěrdwo聽」。第六，中國很早就提-chàng平等。「Shèng-人跟我們是同類的」，「人人都可以作Yáu Shwùn」，都是這個意思。從前每一個念書的人都得背四書。四書裏的這些話對於中國人的影-syǎng很大。第七，四書裏又有一句話說：「在一個國家裏，人民是最重要的，社-jì是第二重要的，hwángdì是最不重要的」。書經這本古書上也有這麽一句話說：「人民是國家的根本。根本結實，國家就平安」。

上面擧出來的這七點，都表現中國這幾千年的民主思想，證明中國是世界上一個很古的民主國家。

(一) 我住在郵政局旁邊兒。樹很多，空氣也很好。

(二) 我的人生觀是：人生是暫時的。誰敢說準甚麽時候死？所以人應當找快樂。

(三) 不管這兒風景多好我也不住，因爲温度變得太快。忽然升高，忽然降低，住久了一定得病。

（四）那個鋪子正在大減價。有各樣的衣服，並且各種各種尺寸都很全。

（五）你先把東西封好包起來。我休息一會兒就帶走。

（六）華先生的性情很好，愛交朋友。我跟他合作，一塊兒造了一條小船。

（七）宗教的勢力很大。社會上一沒宗教就很危險了。這句話是有根據的，不是我隨便亂說。

（八）你別給他介紹女朋友了。他剛結婚。

（九）我發展這個事業，不是爲自己，而是爲我兒子。

Vocabulary

1. 舉 jyǔ　V: raise, lift

　選舉　V/N: elect/election

　舉手　VO: raise the hand

　　一. 這次的選舉，你想選舉誰作總統？

　　二. 誰還不明白，請舉手。

2. 義 yì　BF: meaning; duty

　定義　N: definition

　主義　N: doctrine, -ism

　　一. 民主的定義是甚麼？

　　二. 共產主義跟民主主義有甚麼不同？

3. 被 bèi　CV: by (marking agent in "passive" con-

structions, interchangeable with 叫 and 讓)

一. 我孩子被他孩子打了。

4. 求 chyóu V: beg, seek after

求人 VO: ask for help, ask a favor of someone

一. 我求你幫我一點兒忙。

二. 自己能作的事，千萬別求人。

5. 利 lì BF: gain, profit

利-hai SV: be fierce, severe/(suffix to SVs as an intensive or superlative like 好得利-hai meaning terribly good

一. 他怕太太，因爲聽說他太太很利-hai.

二. 這些日子我忙得利-hai.

6. 存 tswún BF: keep, exist

存在 V: exist

一. 爲人民作事的政府才能存在。

7. 取 chyǔ V: obtain, fetch, take out from

一. 我到城裏去取行李,還取一點兒錢。

8. 消 syāu BF: cancel, diminish

消取 V: cancel, rescind

一. 政府已經决定把這個組織取消了。

9. 制 jr̀ BF: system, regulation

制度 N: system

限制 V/N: limit, restrict/limit, restriction

專制 SV/N: be tyrannous/absolute monarchv

一. 他很專制，限制我們作很多事。

10. 考 kǎu V: examine, test

考書 VO: take an examination (in studies)

考取了 RV: passed an examination

一. 每兩個星期我們考四課書。

二. 那個大學他已經考取了。

11. 試 shr̀ V: test; try

考試 N: an examination

一. 他試了半天還是不行。

二. 今天的考試真難。

12. 參 tsān BF: participate in

參加 V: take part in

參觀 V: pay a visit to (a school, etc.)

一. 我不打算參加這次的考試。

二. 常有人到我們學校來參觀。

13. 將 jyàng/jyāng BF: a general/be about to

古書 MA: in the future

一. 將來我們都有機會到中國去。

14. 古 gǔ SV: be ancient

將來 N: ancient books

15. 受 shòu V: receive; endure

受歡迎 VO: be welcomed

受不了 RV: cannot take, unable to bear

一. 他唱歌兒很受歡迎。

二. 天氣這麼熱，我真受不了。

Mao's birthplace, CHANGSHA: Shaoshan

Notes

1. Lín-肯總統（林-） N: President Lincoln
2. 民有,民治,民-syǎng（享） Ph: "…of the people, by the people and for the people"—lit. people own, people govern and people enjoy
3. 管理 V: manage
   一. 政府管理人民的事。
4. fú-利（福-） N: welfare
5. 封建制度 N: feudalism
6. jyējí（階級） N: caste, class
7. "將相本無種" Ph: "There is no blood in generals or premiers, "meaning everybody can be a general or a premier（相 is pronounced <u>syàng</u> here）
8. hwángdì（皇帝） N: emperor
9. "受命於天" Ph: mandate is from Heaven—lit. receive appointment from Heaven
10. 治理 V: rule, govern
    治理-chywán(-權) N: the right to rule
11. 自動的 A: automatically
    一. 他可以請我去。我不能自動的去。
12. 革命 V/N: revolt/revolution
    一. 政府不好，人民就可以革命。
    二. 法國有過三次革命。
13. Yùshř（御史） N: a censor（whose duty was to keep the emperor informed and advise him on all matters of importance）
14. jyānchá（監察） V: inspect, examine
15. "天由人民的yǎnjing看, Ph: (the original quotation from 書經,

由人民的ěrdwo聽" the Book of History, is:) "天視自我民視，天聽自我民聽" — 視 is pronounced shr̀; the characters for yǎnjing and ěrdwo are 眼睛 and 耳朵 respectively, 睛 and 朵 are pronounced like jīng and dwǒ respectively when stressed

16. 平等 SV/N: be equal /equality

一. 他不能在這兒買房子是很不平等的一件事。

二. 人人都愛自由跟平等。

17. shèng‧人 (聖人‧) N: a sage, saint

同類 N: of the same species — the original quotation from Mencius is: "聖人與我同類者", 與 and 者 are pronounced yǔ and jě respectively

18. Yáu Shwùn (堯舜) N: Yao and Shun, two legendary sage emperors who are said to have reigned 2357-2255 B.C. and 2255-2205 B.C. respectively — the original quotation from Mencius is:
"人皆可以爲堯舜"; 皆 is pronounced jyē

19. 四書 N: the Four Books: (1) Dàsywé (大學), the Great Learning, (2) Jūngyūng (中庸), Doctrine of the Mean, (3) Lwúnyǔ (論語), Confucian Analects, (4) Mèngdž (孟子), Mencius

一. 從前中國人小時候都念四書。

20. 社‧jì (‧稷) N: one's country — the original quotation

from Mencius is: "民爲貴，社稷次之，君爲輕" 君 and 輕 are pronounced jyūn and chīng respectively

21. 根本 N: root, foundation—the original quotation from 書經, the Book of History, reads: "民爲邦本,本固邦寧"; 邦, 固 and 寧 are pronounced bāng, gù and níng respectively

22. 結實 SV: be strong, durable

一. 他很結實，可是他太太常有病。

23. 證明 V/N: certify/a proof

一. 你能證明他今天真有病嗎？

二. 我沒有甚麼證明。你必得信我的話。

24. 人生觀 N: philosophy of life

一. 人人都有人生觀，可是有人說不出來他的人生觀是甚麼。

25. 快樂 SV/N: be happy / happiness (pronounced kwàilè)

一. 他的生活很快樂。

二. 人活着應當找快樂。

26. 減價 VO: reduce the price

一. 這個地方減價三天。快去買吧。

"ASSUMED" CHARACTER LIST
(300 basic characters from Read Chinese, Book One)

1 - 3 STROKES	ROMANIZATION	LESSON	也	yě	1	比	bǐ	17	北	běi	18
一	yī	1	山	shān	17	水	shwěi	13	叫	jyàu	6
又	yòu	8	千	chyān	10	中	jūng	1	四	sz̀	1
二	èr	1	女	nyǔ	10	今	jīn	7	出	chū	8
十	shŕ	1	4			分	fēn	13	外	wài	2
七	chī	1	火	hwǒ	13	父	fù	7	母	mǔ	7
了	le <lyǎu>	2	六	lyòu	1	月	ywè	1	生	shēng	3
人	rén	1	文	wén	16	手	shǒu	10	用	yùng	4
八	bā	1	方	fāng	2	毛	máu	19	句	jyù	11
九	jyǒu	1	心	syīn	19	5			白	bái	13
三	sān	1	王	wáng	19	半	bàn	6	他	tā	1
已	yǐ	13	天	tyān	1	必	bì	11	6		
己	jǐ	14	夫	fū	14	平	píng	15	字	dz̀	5
下	syà	1	五	wǔ	1	打	dǎ	14	忙	máng	18
工	gūng	14	太	tài	9	可	kě	4	次	tsz̀	17
子	dž	3	友	yǒu	6	正	jèng	11	衣	yī	16
才	tsái	19	不	bù	1	去	chyù	3	有	yǒu	1
大	dà	1	少	shǎu	3	本	běn	5	百	bǎi	6
小	syǎu	1	以	yǐ	5	左	dzwǒ	18	在	dzài	2
上	shàng	1	日	r̀	5	右	yòu	18	西	syī	4

老	lǎu	6	忘	wàng	12	近	jìn	18	奇	chí	19
再	dzài	8	那	nà	2	8			到	dàu	2
地	dı	2	車	chē	13	河	hé	17	呢	ne	11
早	dzǎu	6	更	gèng	17	法	fà <fá>	16	門	mén	8
因	yīn	9	把	bǎ	8	定	dìng	11	明	míng	7
吃	chr̄	5	找	jǎu	13	怪	gwài	19	易	yì	16
回	hwéi	5	走	dzǒu	6	怕	pà	16	些	syē	4
名	míng	16	見	jyàn	11	房	fáng	10	念	nyàn	7
多	dwō	3	吧	ba	11	放	fàng	14	朋	péng	6
年	nyán	8	別	byé	9	夜	yè	12	知	jr̄	8
先	syān	3	男	nán	10	底	dǐ	14	兒	ér	2
自	dz̀	14	坐	dzwò	5	刻	kè	13	的	de <dì>	1
件	jyàn	9	告	gàu	12	長	cháng	17	所	swǒ	7
好	hǎu	3	我	wǒ	1	玩	wán	15	姓	syìng	7
行	syíng	9	每	měi	19	表	byǎu	10	往	wàng	19
7			位	wèi	9	事	shr̀	4	9		
沒	méi	1	住	jù	7	東	dūng	4	洗	syǐ	19
完	wán	16	你	nǐ	1	兩	lyǎng	1	送	sùng	9
弟	dì	12	但	dàn	19	直	jŕ	18	差	chà	13
快	kwài	8	作	dzwò	4	來	lái	3	美	měi	16

前	chyán	2	10			們	mén	1	夠	gòu	15
穿	chwān	18	酒	jyǒu	18	個	gè	1	魚	yú	17
客	kè	16	家	jyā	7	候	hòu	4	進	jìn	9
為	wèi <wéi>	6	容	rúng	16	條	tyáu	17	船	chwán	17
屋	wū	10	站	jàn	12	紙	jř	10	得	děi <dé>	13
孩	hái	12	這	jè	2	11			從	tsúng	8
城	chéng	12	高	gāu	11	着	je <jáu>	8	12		
要	yàu	3	病	bìng	15	情	chíng	9	道	dàu	8
南	nán	18	書	shū	7	許	syǔ	19	訴	sùng <sù>	12
甚	shém <shèn>	2	哥	gē	15	張	jāng	11	就	jyòu	5
是	shr̀	1	起	chǐ	8	現	syàn	6	畫	hwà	17
昨	dzwó	7	真	jēn	10	教	jyāu <jyàu>	13	報	bàu	13
思	sz̄	9	校	syàu	14	都	dōu <dū>	4	喜	syǐ	15
怎	dzěn	11	時	shŕ	4	帶	dài	15	極	jí	17
拜	bài	9	哭	kū	15	常	cháng	10	桌	jwō	14
看	kàn	3	茶	chá	14	問	wèn	5	黑	hēi	17
信	syìn	10	笑	syàu	14	晚	wǎn	7	最	dzwèi	17
便	byàn <pyán>	19	拿	ná	9	唱	chàng	11	開	kāi	13
很	hěn	3	能	néng	5	國	gwó	3	喝	hē	18
後	hòu	2	氣	chì	11	第	dì	1	貴	gwèi	9

跑	pǎu	13	當	dāng	15	請	chǐng	5	幫	bāng	15
過	gwò	13	睡	shwèi	15	誰	shéi	10	點	dyǎn	6
菜	tsài	14	跟	gēn	11	賣	mài	4	臉	lyǎn	19
買	mǎi	4	路	lù	15	樣	yàng	17	18~		
飯	fàn	5	萬	wàn	10	數	shù	19	識	shr̀	14
筆	bǐ	10	歲	swèi	12	鋪	pù	16	離	lí	18
等	děng	8	愛	ài	9	16			壞	hwài	16
然	rán	19	會	hwèi	5	懂	dǔng	12	聽	tīng	6
短	dwǎn	17	經	jīng	13	親	chīn	7	願	ywàn	15
給	gěi	3	14			辦	bàn	16	關	gwān	13
幾	jǐ	6	慢	màn	8	頭	tóu	2	歡	hwān	15
街	jyē	12	說	shwō	3	還	hái <hwán>	6	舊	jyòu	18
13			認	rèn	14	館	gwǎn	18	難	nán	13
新	syīn	10	麼	ma	2	錯	tswò	16	鐘	jūng	8
意	yì	6	歌	gē	11	錢	chyán	4	覺	jywé <jyàu>	16
話	hwà	3	緊	jǐn	11	學	sywé	5	邊	byān	18
裏	lǐ	2	對	dwèi	4	17					
遠	ywǎn	18	算	swàn	14	謝	syè	5			
塊	kwài	7	15			禮	lǐ	9			
想	syǎng	4	寫	syě	5	應	yīng	15			

BASIC STROKE FORMS

六	月	己
火	吃	我
河	又	心
大	近	字
這	十	人
三	水	千
完	很	去
打	山	女

SOME SUGGESTIONS ON WRITING AND PRINCIPLES OF STROKE FORMATION

In writing Chinese characters, it is important to observe certain principles of stroke order evolved from the experience of many generations of Chinese calligraphers. Important as they are, these principles are very general in nature and people do differ in minor details. Just as many an American would say, 'Nobody is going to tell me whether to write the horizontal or the vertical line first in the capital letter T,' the Chinese people can be equally stubborn in this matter. Listed below are seven of the most generally observed principles.

1. From upper left-hand corner to lower right-hand corner. This is an over-all principle, embracing the remaining six, and guides the writing of all characters not covered by them (see illustrations 1 to 6).
2. From left to right, as in 八 (see illustration 1).
3. From top to bottom, as in 二 (see illustration 2).
4. From outside to inside, as in 日 (see illustration 3). Note how the inside is filled in first before the base line is added.
5. Horizontal before other lines crossing it, as in 十 (see illustration 4).
6. Slanting stroke to the left before the one to the right, as in 父 (see illustration 5).
7. Center stroke before its symmetrical wings, as in 小 (see illustration 6).

	ILLUSTRATION	STROKE ORDER			
1	八	ノ	八		
2	二	一	二		
3	日	丨	冂	月	日
4	十	一	十		
5	父	ノ	ハ	㐅	父
6	小	亅	亅	小	

Supplementary illustrations to show the Principles of stroke order, and direction of each stroke.

Illustration 1 Illustration 2 Illustration 3
Illustration 4 Illustration 5 Illustration 6

The number of strokes in a certain character sometimes differs from one writer to another, and even from one dictionary to another. In debatable cases, arbitrary determination of the number of strokes, based on common usage, has been made by the author in order to avoid unnecessary problems for the beginning student.

In the following list, if the written form differs from the printed form, the former is used.

CHARACTER INDEX

The index below lists all the required characters introduced in READ ABOUT CHINA. It does not list the characters listed in the Notes section of each lesson. The required characters are arranged by <u>total</u> stroke count. To find a character you must count the total number of strokes <u>carefully</u>. If you fail to find the character, recount the strokes and search again. You might also try looking for the character among those with one stroke more or one stroke less than the number of strokes you have totalled for the character.

As an aid to correct stroke count we note here some elements of characters (chiefly certain radicals) whose stroke count is sometimes difficult to perceive:

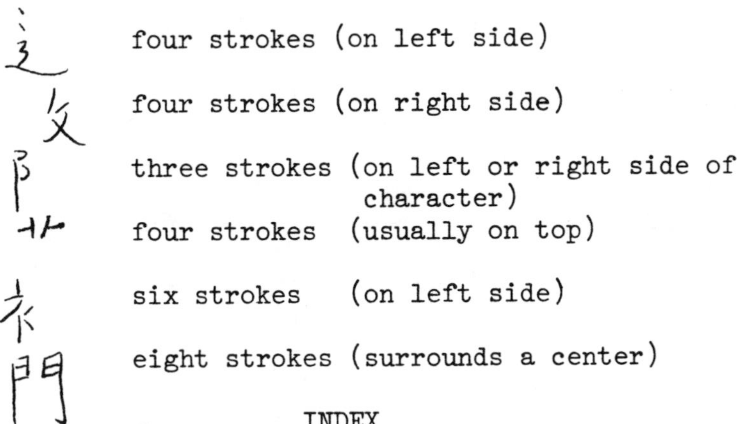

- 辶 four strokes (on left side)
- 攵 four strokes (on right side)
- 阝 three strokes (on left or right side of character)
- 艹 four strokes (usually on top)
- 衤 six strokes (on left side)
- 門 eight strokes (surrounds a center)

INDEX

In this Index we list first the character (arranged according to total stroke count), then the pronunciation (Yale romanization), and finally the page reference where the character and its definition is explained.

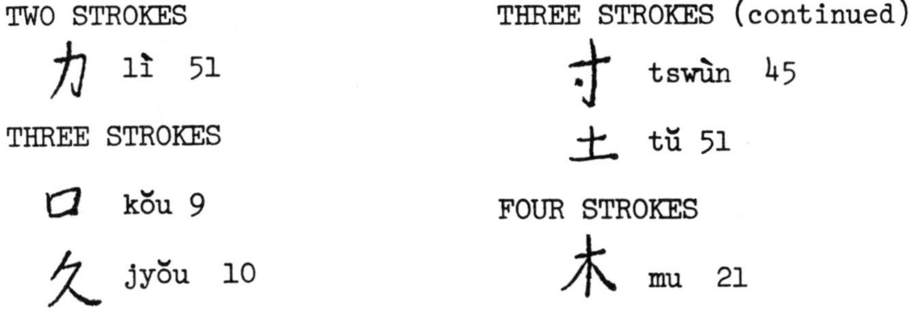

TWO STROKES

力 lì 51

THREE STROKES

口 kǒu 9

久 jyǒu 10

THREE STROKES (continued)

寸 tswùn 45

土 tǔ 51

FOUR STROKES

木 mu 21

FOUR STROKES (continued)

切 chyè 26
介 jyè 44
内 nèi 80
尺 chř 88
公 gūng 88
反 fǎn 96
升 shēng 102
化 hwà 110
片 pyàn 117
午 wǔ 117

FIVE STROKES

世 shř 3
只 jř 4
民 mín 9
且 chyě 16
皮 pí 20
石 shŕ 21
代 dài 26
包 bāu 38
另 lìng 38
加 jyā 62

FIVE STROKES (continued)

主 jǔ 62
由 yóu 68
永 yǔng 69
立 lì 81
市 shř 96
冬 dūng 116
古 gǔ 124

SIX STROKES

共 gùng 4
江 jyāng 9
全 chywán 9
各 gè 16
成 chéng 21
休 syōu 31
式 shř 31
收 shōu 32
死 sž 37
米 mǐ 38
安 ān 45
光 gwāng 45
合 hé 51

SIX STROKES (continued)

危 wēi,wéi 52
同 túng 57
如 rú 62
向 syàng 63
而 ér 68
丢 dyōu 69
任 rèn 74
交 jyāu 89
此 tsž 95
低 dī 102
色 sè 103
決 jywé 109
肉 ròu 117
存 tswún 123
考 kǎu 123

SEVEN STROKES

佔 jàn 15
希 syī 25
改 gǎi 38
究 jyōu 56
李 lǐ 57
社 shè 68

SEVEN STROKES (continued)

何 hé 74
助 jù 80
努 nǔ 81
形 syíng 102
局 jyú 103
困 kwùn 109
身 shēn 116
冷 lěng 116
利 lì 123
求 chyóu 123

EIGHT STROKES

並 bìng 16
非 fēi 16
於 yú 20
步 bù 21
花 hwā 31
或 hwò 38
金 jīn 45
妹 mèi 57
姐 jyě 58
官 gwān 62
性 syìng 62
命 mìng 69

EIGHT STROKES (con't)

宗	dzūng	70
注	jù	69
迎	yíng	70
府	fǔ	74
果	gwǒ	75
使	shř	75
味	wèi	75
服	fú	81
青	chīng	81
治	jr̀	89
彼	bǐ	95
其	chí	95
忽	hū	102
空	kūng	103
典	dyǎn	110
革	gé	110
肯	kěn	116
取	chyǔ	123
制	jr̀	123
受	shòu	124

NINE STROKES

故	gu	3
界	jyè	3
面	myàn	4
洋	yáng	4
亮	lyàng	15
重	jùng	20
活	hwó	20
紀	jì	20
紅	húng	26
封	fēng	26
音	yīn	31
春	chwūn	32
風	fēng	37
俗	sú	37
秋	chyōu	38
厚	hòu	52
研	yán	56
背	bèi	57
專	jwān	62
按	àn	62
保	bǎu	62

NINE STROKES (con't)

度 dù 68
政 jèng 74
派 pài 80
相 syāng 82
建 jyàn 87
省 shěng 88
查 chá 110
限 syàn 110
星 syīng 117

TEN STROKES

原 ywán 3
海 hǎi 3
連 lyán 4
特 tè 4
除 chú 9
恐 kǔng 25
花 hwā 31
息 syí 31
馬 mǎ 32
殺 shā 37

TEN STROKES (con't)

記 jì 44
留 lyóu 44
救 jyòu 45
倍 bèi 51
剛 gāng 52
旁 páng 62
借 jyè 63
展 jǎn 69
祖 dzǔ 69
神 shén 74
根 gēn 75
院 ywàn 81
修 syōu 88
夏 syà 116
既 jì 116
消 syāu 123

ELEVEN STROKES

部 bù 3
淨 jìng 9
商 shāng 9

ELEVEN STROKES (con't)

乾 gān 9
產 chǎn 10
敢 gǎn 16
造 dzàu 20
望 wàng 25
陰 yīn 25
接 jyē 26
通 tūng 32
處 chù 37
涼 lyáng 38
理 lǐ 44
紹 shàu 44
清 chīng 44
停 tíng 51
婚 hwūn 58
習 syí 58
規 gwēi 63
迎 yíng 70
細 syì 74
設 shè 81
務 wù 81
動 dùng 82
推 twēi 96
貨 hwò 96
您 nín 102
降 jyàng 102
組 dzǔ 109
假 jyà 117
被 bèi 122
將 jyāng 124
參 tsān 124

TWELVE STROKES

黃 hwang 3
湖 hú 9
發 fā 15
越 ywè 16
備 bèi 25
陽 yáng 25
普 pǔ 32
間 jyān 45

TWELVE STROKES (con't)

無 wú 51
量 lyàng 51
單 dān 57
景 jĭng 57
結 jyé 57
華 hwá 62
鄉 syāng 63
替 tì 69
費 fèi 95
統 tŭng 96
答 dá 96
減 jyăn 102
郵 yóu 103
提 tí 110
溫 wēn 116
期 chī 117

THIRTEEN STROKES

業 yè 9
準 jwŭn 10
傳 chwán 15

THIRTEEN STROKES (con't)

運 yùn 15
預 yù 25
號 hàu 25
電 dyàn 32
跳 tyàu 37
圓 yuăn 38
楚 chŭ 44
詳 syáng 74
亂 lwàn 80
寬 kwān 88
勢 shr̀ 95
圍 wéi 95
照 jàu 102
解 jyĕ 109
該 gāi 117
義 yì 122
試 shr̀ 124

FOURTEEN STROKES

種 jŭng 15
像 syàng 15
管 gwăn 44

FOURTEEN STROKES (con't)

稱 chēng 62
精 jīng 81
語 yǔ 95
滿 mǎn 109
聞 wén 116
與 jyǔ 122

FIFTEEN STROKES

課 kè 3
暫 jàn 10
整 jěng 20
談 tán 21
熱 rè 25
鬧 nàu 25
論 lwùn 51
賤 jyàn 51
概 gài 52
實 shŕ 56
價 jyà 74
影 yǐng 74
靠 kàu 87
模 mwò 88
餘 yú 95
範 fàn 95
樂 ywè 103
線 syàn 103
複 fù 109

SIXTEEN STROKES

樹 shù 20
據 jyù 21
燈 dēng 31
隨 swéi 51
險 syǎn 52
選 sywǎn 57
機 jī 74
縣 syàn 88

SEVENTEEN STROKES

總 dzǔng 3
講 jyǎng 15
雖 swéi 15
聲 shēng 31

SEVENTEEN STROKES (con't)

牆 chyáng 87

EIGHTEEN STROKES

類 lèi 31

題 tí 38

簡 jyǎn 57

醫 yī 81

織 jř 109

雜 dzá 109

NINETEEN STROKES

證 jèng 103

TWENTY OR MORE STROKES

黨 dǎng 10

變 byàn 21

讓 ràng 31

勸 chywàn 45

觀 gwān 68

體 tǐ 69

護 hù 88

鐵 tyě 89

屬 shǔ 109

COMPARATIVE TRANSCRIPTION TABLE

Yale Wade-Giles Pinyin

Yale	Wade-Giles	Pinyin	Yale	Wade-Giles	Pinyin
a	a	a	chye	ch'ieh	qie
ai	ai	ai	chyou	ch'iu	qiu
an	an	an	chyu	ch'ü	qu
ang	ang	ang	chyun	ch'ün	qun
au	ao	ao	chyung	ch'iung	qiong
			chywan	ch'üan	quan
ba	pa	ba	chywe	ch'üeh	que
bai	pai	bai			
ban	pan	ban	da	ta	da
bang	pang	bang	dai	tai	dai
bau	pao	bao	dan	tan	dan
bei	pei	bei	dang	tang	dang
ben	pen	ben	dau	tao	dao
beng	peng	beng	de	te	de
bi	pi	bi	dei	tei	dei
bin	pin	bin	deng	teng	deng
bing	ping	bing	di	ti	di
bou	pou	bou	ding	ting	ding
bu	pu	bu	dou	tou	dou
bwo	po	bo	du	tu	du
byan	pien	bian	dung	tung	dong
byau	piao	biao	dwan	tuan	duan
bye	pieh	bie	dwei	tui	dui
			dwo	to	duo
cha	ch'a	cha	dwun	tun	dun
chai	ch'ai	chai	dyan	tien	dian
chan	ch'an	chan	dyau	tiao	diao
chang	ch'ang	chang	dye	tieh	die
chau	ch'ao	chao	dyou	tiu	diu
che	ch'e	che	dz	tzu	zi
chen	ch'en	chen	dza	tsa	za
cheng	ch'eng	cheng	dzai	tsai	zai
chi	ch'i	qi	dzan	tsan	zan
chir	ch'in	qin	dzang	tsang	zang
chi'	ch'ing	qing	dzau	tsao	zao
chc	ch'ou	chou	dze	tse	ze
chı	ch'ih	chi	dzei	tsei	zei
chu	ch'u	chu	dzen	tsen	zen
chung	ch'ung	chong	dzeng	tseng	zeng
chwai	ch'uai	chuai	dzou	tsou	zou
chwan	ch'uan	chuan	dzu	tsu	zu
chwang	ch'uang	chuang	dzung	tsung	zong
chwei	ch'ui	chui	dzwan	tsuan	zuan
chwo	ch'o	chuo	dzwei	tsui	zui
chwun	ch'un	chun	dzwo	tso	zuo
chya	ch'ia	qia	dzwun	tsun	zun
chyan	ch'ien	qian			
chyang	ch'iang	qiang	e	e, o	e
chyau	ch'iao	qiao	ei	ei	ei

Yale	Wade-Giles	Pinyin
en	en	en
eng	eng	eng
er	erh	er
fa	fa	fa
fan	fan	fan
fang	fang	fang
fei	fei	fei
fen	fen	fen
feng	feng	feng
fou	fou	fou
fu	fu	fu
fwo	fo	fo
ga	ka	ga
gai	kai	gai
gan	kan	gan
gang	kang	gang
gau	kao	gao
ge	ke, ko	ge
gei	kei	gei
gen	ken	gen
geng	keng	geng
gou	kou	gou
gu	ku	gu
gung	kung	gong
gwa	kua	gua
gwai	kuai	guai
gwan	kuan	guan
gwang	kuang	guang
gwei	kuei	gui
gwo	kuo	guo
gwun	kun	gun
ha	ha	ha
hai	hai	hai
han	han	han
hang	hang	hang
hau	hao	hao
he	ho	he
hei	hei	hei
hen	hen	hen
heng	heng	heng
hou	hou	hou
hu	hu	hu
hung	hung	hong
hwa	hua	hua
hwai	huai	huai
hwan	huan	huan
hwang	huang	huang
hwei	hui	hui
hwo	huo	huo
hwun	hun	hun
ja	cha	zha
jai	chai	zhai
jan	chan	zhan
jang	chang	zhang

Yale	Wade-Giles	Pinyin
jau	chao	zhao
je	che	zhe
jei	chei	zhei
jen	chen	zhen
jeng	cheng	zheng
ji	chi	ji
jin	chin	jin
jing	ching	jing
jou	chou	zhou
jr	chih	zhi
ju	chu	zhu
jung	chung	zhong
jwa	chua	zhua
jwai	chuai	zhuai
jwan	chuan	zhuan
jwang	chuang	zhuang
jwei	chui	zhui
jwo	cho	zhuo
jwun	chun	zhun
jya	chia	jia
jyan	chien	jian
jyang	chiang	jiang
jyau	chiao	jiao
jye	chieh	jie
jyou	chiu	jiu
jyu	chü	ju
jyun	chün	jun
jyung	chiung	jiong
jywan	chüan	juan
jywe	chüeh	jue
ka	k'a	ka
kai	k'ai	kai
kan	k'an	kan
kang	k'ang	kang
kau	k'ao	kao
ke	k'e, k'o	ke
ken	k'en	ken
keng	k'eng	keng
kou	k'ou	kou
ku	k'u	ku
kung	k'ung	kong
kwa	k'ua	kua
kwai	k'uai	kuai
kwan	k'uan	kuan
kwang	k'uang	kuang
kwei	k'uei	kui
kwo	k'uo	kuo
kwun	k'un	kun
la	la	la
lai	lai	lai
lan	lan	lan
lang	lang	lang
lau	lao	lao
le	le	le
lei	lei	lei
leng	leng	leng

Yale	Wade-Giles	Pinyin
li	li	li
lin	lin	lin
ling	ling	ling
lou	lou	lou
lu	lu	lu
lung	lung	long
lwan	luan	luan
lwo	lo	luo
lwun	lun	lun
lya	lia	lia
lyan	lien	lian
lyang	liang	liang
lyau	liao	liao
lye	lieh	lie
lyou	liu	liu
lyu	lü	lü
lywan	lüan	lüan
lywe	lüeh	lüe
ma	ma	ma
mai	mai	mai
man	man	man
mang	mang	mang
mau	mao	mao
mei	mei	mei
men	men	men
meng	meng	meng
mi	mi	mi
min	min	min
ming	ming	ming
mou	mou	mou
mu	mu	mu
mwo	mo	mo
myan	mien	mian
myau	miao	miao
mye	mieh	mie
myou	miu	miu
na	na	na
nai	nai	nai
nan	nan	nan
nang	nang	nang
nau	nao	nao
ne	ne	ne
nei	nei	nei
nen	nen	nen
neng	neng	neng
ni	ni	ni
nin	nin	nin
ning	ning	ning
nou	nou	nou
nu	nu	nu
nung	nung	nong
nwan	nuan	nuan
nwo	no	nuo
nwun	nun	nun
nyan	nien	nian
nyang	niang	niang

Yale	Wade-Giles	Pinyin
nyau	niao	niao
nye	nieh	nie
nyou	niu	niu
nyu	nü	nü
nywe	nüeh	nüe
ou	ou	ou
pa	p'a	pa
pai	p'ai	pai
pan	p'an	pan
pang	p'ang	pang
pau	p'ao	pao
pei	p'ei	pei
pen	p'en	pen
peng	p'eng	peng
pi	p'i	pi
pin	p'in	pin
ping	p'ing	ping
pou	p'ou	pou
pu	p'u	pu
pwo	p'o	po
pyan	p'ien	pian
pyau	p'iao	piao
pye	p'ieh	pie
r	jih	ri
ran	jan	ran
rang	jang	rang
rau	jao	rao
re	je	re
ren	jen	ren
reng	jeng	reng
rou	jou	rou
ru	ju	ru
rung	jung	rong
rwan	juan	ruan
rwei	jui	rui
rwo	jo	ruo
rwun	jun	run
sa	sa	sa
sai	sai	sai
san	san	san
sang	sang	sang
sau	sao	sao
se	se	se
sen	sen	sen
seng	seng	seng
sha	sha	sha
shai	shai	shai
shan	shan	shan
shang	shang	shang
shau	shao	shao
she	she	she
shei	shei	shei
shen	shen	shen
sheng	sheng	sheng

Yale	Wade-Giles	Pinyin	Yale	Wade-Giles	Pinyin
shou	shou	shou	tsau	ts'ao	cao
shr	shih	shi	tse	ts'e	ce
shu	shu	shu	tsen	ts'en	cen
shwa	shua	shua	tseng	ts'eng	ceng
shwai	shuai	shuai	tsou	ts'ou	cou
shwan	shuan	shuan	tsu	ts'u	cu
shwang	shuang	shuang	tsung	ts'ung	cong
shwei	shui	shui	tswan	ts'uan	cuan
shwo	shuo	shuo	tswei	ts'ui	cui
shwun	shun	shun	tswo	ts'o	cuo
sou	sou	sou	tswun	ts'un	cun
su	su	su	tsz	tz'u	ci
sung	sung	song	tu	t'u	tu
swan	suan	suan	tung	t'ung	tong
swei	sui	sui	twan	t'uan	tuan
swo	so	suo	twei	t'ui	tui
swun	sun	sun	two	t'o	tuo
sya	hsia	xia	twun	t'un	tun
syan	hsien	xian	tyan	t'ien	tian
syang	hsiang	xiang	tyau	t'iao	tiao
syau	hsiao	xiao	tye	t'ieh	tie
sye	hsieh	xie			
syi	hsi	xi	wa	wa	wa
syin	hsin	xin	wai	wai	wai
sying	hsing	xing	wan	wan	wan
syou	hsiu	xiu	wang	wang	wang
syu	hsü	xu	wei	wei	wei
syun	hsün	xun	wen	wen	wen
syung	hsiung	xiong	weng	weng	weng
sywan	hsüan	xuan	wo	wo	wo
sywe	hsüeh	xue	wu	wu	wu
sz	ssu, szu	si			
			ya	ya	ya
ta	t'a	ta	yai	yai	yai
tai	t'ai	tai	yan	yen	yan
tan	t'an	tan	yang	yang	yang
tang	t'ang	tang	yau	yao	yao
tau	t'ao	tao	ye	yeh	ye
te	t'e	te	yi	yi, i	yi
teng	t'eng	teng	yin	yin	yin
ti	t'i	ti	ying	ying	ying
ting	t'ing	ting	you	yu	you
tou	t'ou	tou	yu	yü	yu
tsa	ts'a	ca	yun	yün	yun
tsai	ts'ai	cai	yung	yung	yong
tsan	ts'an	can	ywan	yüan	yuan
tsang	ts'ang	cang	ywe	yüeh	yue